Contents

Contents

African and Caribbean Celebrations

Gail Johnson

Illustrated by Caroline Glanville
Edited by Toby Green

Hawthorn Press

Published by Hawthorn Press, Hawthorn House,
1 Lansdown Lane, Stroud, Gloucestershire, GL5 1BJ, UK
Tel: (01453) 757040 Fax: (01453) 751138
email: info@hawthornpress.com
Website: **www.hawthornpress.com**

Drawings and cover illustration © Caroline Glanville
Cover design by Hawthorn Press, Stroud, Gloucestershire
Design and typesetting by Lynda Smith at Hawthorn Press, Stroud, Gloucestershire
Printed by Butler and Tanner, Frome, Somerset

Mixed Sources
Product group from well-managed
forests and other controlled sources
www.fsc.org Cert no. SGS-COC-1722
© 1996 Forest Stewardship Council
FSC

Henna and mehndi patterns adapted from traditional designs.
Marriage à la Mode: IV, The Toilette, c.1743 (oil on canvas) by William Hogarth, (1697-1764) © National Gallery, London, UK/The Bridgeman Art Library. Nationality/copyright status: English/out of copyright
Slave plantation society from *The Caribbean Experience: An Historical Survey, 1450-1960*, Douglas Hall, 1982. Reprinted by permission of Harcourt Education.
Che-che-koo-lay music and lyrics from *Mantra's Multicultural Book of Songs*, Misha Chadha, 1994, reproduced by kind permission of Mantra Lingua Ltd.
Redrawing of Arms of Jamaica (Coat of Arms) and explanation of its provenance granted by kind permission of The Office of the Prime Minister, Jamaica.
'Terrapin's Pot of Sense' and 'Anansi's Pot of Wisdom' from the book *A Treasury of Afro-American Folklore* by Harold Courlander, Copyright © 1976, 1996 by Harold Courlander. Appears by permission of the publisher, Marlowe & Company, A Division of Avalon Publishing Group, Inc.
'Anancy' from *Tales of the Caribbean* by Andrew Salkey, published by Ginn and Company Ltd., 1985.
'Education is a must' by Slinger Francisco, The Mighty Sparrow, Calypso King of the World, published by Sparrow Music.
'I like to stay up' from *I like that stuff* Copyright © Grace Nichols, 1984, reproduced with permission of Curtis Brown Group Ltd.

Every effort has been made to trace the ownership of all copyrighted material and to acknowledge this. If any omission as been made, please bring this to the attention of the publisher so that proper acknowledgement can be made in future editions.

British Library Cataloguing in Publication Data applied for

ISBN 978-1-903458-00-6

Contents

Acknowledgements

I am grateful to so many people, friends and family, who assisted and encouraged me in the writing of this book. I thank them for their time and patience, and for sharing their knowledge and experiences.

Particular thanks to:
Lis McDermott, Howard Francis, Paul Mathurin, Venet Johnson, Ben Baddoo, Ropert McKenzie, Annet Richards-Binns, Carlton Green, Jane Grell, Denise Taitt, Kaushar Ussenbai, Tony Miller, Patience Tsapko, Tommy Pierson, Hyacinth Lewis and Julian Shaw.

Foreword

I am amazed looking back some 40 years at how absolutely clear I was about my identity as an African of Caribbean extraction, Jamaican to be precise, in England. That sense of identity was unambivalent, firmly grounded in my upbringing within an extended and proud family. I excelled at school. Although my primary school teachers were not black, we felt cared for and loved, and the teachers' ignorance of our background did not negate the character-building that took place in our homes and our churches. I spent very happy and formative years in those primary school classrooms. In many ways, our teachers affirmed the values of my parents and grandparents.

My secondary school experience was very different. Here my teachers would have enhanced their considerable capacity as educators had such tools as this book been at their disposal. If they could have drawn on such a book it would, firstly, have created a space for the few of us African Caribbean students who managed to slip through the colour-bar net to feel comfortable in our own skins. Secondly, it would have given us and our fellow students a greater understanding of the continent that gave birth to the human race and of everyone's connection to it. None of my classical studies ever touched on the African continent, and so I underwent a 'schooling' process at secondary level that had little to do with 'educare', the Latin verb to lead or bring out, that which was within me. My collision with my African self was far from affirming or celebratory in this environment. For the first time in my life I felt like a spectator in my classroom, peering only periodically and partially at myself through a mirror darkly, and never quite at ease with either the angle or the definition of what was reflected back.

Now as I educate the educators and school leaders of tomorrow I marvel at how little some parents and teachers know about themselves, never mind the children they are collectively raising, or the realities of the world for which they are preparing them. Teachers of all backgrounds often ask me about resources that they can use that positively and accurately reflect the cultures of the children in their classrooms. We continue in the 21st century to seek authentic and honest resources that will move African Caribbean children away from the sidelines to become active participants in a truly educational process and provide them with the same sense of identity that I had as child. Every child should emerge from compulsory education first and foremost with a real sense of who they are, from where they have come and their limitless potential. Parents too are glad these days to have a reference point for the traditions that they want to be able to pass on, often without appreciating their historical roots.

This resource is a succulent entrée, an accessible starting point for beginning to understand and celebrate the richness and diversity of the culture and traditions of a unique group of people, among whom I count myself: those of African Caribbean ancestry, wherever we may find ourselves in the diaspora.

Rosemary Campbell-Stephens
Consultant
University of London, Institute of Education

In memory of my father, Byron Thompson
and my brother, Andrew Thompson,
and for the next generation, my daughters Kathryn and Sara.

Introduction

This book contains a wealth of information and practical ideas for activities that bring learning to life! It includes both historical information and much that is contemporary. Some of the information may be completely new to readers, while other aspects may provide more understanding of a particular African or Caribbean tradition already known to them. The book aims to look at individual topics in depth, as well as providing an overview of important aspects of African-Caribbean culture. If you want to explore Carnival and the music of a steel band, or to understand why a local Jamaican family throws a party after a family member has died, this book is for you. I hope that both experts and novices will find useful things here.

The book is divided into four sections: *The Historical Background*; *Festivals and Food*; *Music, Dance and the Oral Tradition*; and *Rites of Passage*. The first section gives the background to everything covered in the remainder of the book. The other three parts, however, contain a mixture of factual information and ideas for using this information constructively in a learning environment, with ideas for games and activities appropriate to particular times of year. Here you will find anecdotes from individuals who have experienced particular festivals, traditions or customs, extracts from novels and autobiographies, recipes, games, crafts and ideas for extension activities. In each part, the reader moves from traditions based in Africa to those from the Caribbean, the aim being to mirror the movement of the diaspora of African peoples.

On being asked to write a book about African and Caribbean Celebrations, or customs and traditions, it seemed an impossible task. Where was one to start and to finish? Africa is a huge continent, and the Caribbean consists of a myriad of islands which have as many differences as they have similarities. Inevitably, choices have had to be made, and some people may regret the omissions. This volume is, therefore, merely a taste of the tremendously rich and varied traditions of the African diaspora. Nevertheless we hope that it will serve as a springboard for readers' own further exploration. Useful references, websites and a bibliography are provided to assist in this purpose.

Who is this book for?

Teachers who wish to enrich the curriculum they currently provide for all pupils will find this book especially useful for children aged between 8 and 12. The aim is to make that curriculum more inclusive through the creation of relevant and meaningful learning opportunities for children of African and Caribbean descent. The book can also serve as a tool to assist in teaching the value of diversity and for challenging racism. Moreover, exploring aspects of African and Caribbean culture may quite simply help teachers to gain a better understanding of the pupils they teach and their families.

Teaching opportunities across the breadth of the National Curriculum abound for teachers of all Key Stages, but in particular Key Stages 2, 3 and 4. Many of the activities cut across the curriculum to meet the learning needs of children, covering the five areas of: literacy, numeracy, creativity, ICT and education for sustainable development.

In particular, however, they are adaptable under the National Curriculum areas of:

English – with opportunities for speaking and listening, discussion, looking at Standard English and language variations, reading and writing.

History – with opportunities for chronological understanding, knowledge and understanding of events, people and changes in the past, historical enquiry, and organisation and communication. Starting points for Local history and World history studies can also be found.

Art and Design – with opportunities for exploring and developing ideas, investigating and making art, craft and design, evaluating and developing work, knowledge and understanding.

Design and Technology – with opportunities for developing, planning and communicating ideas, working with tools, equipment, materials and components to make quality products, evaluating processes and products, knowledge and understanding of materials and components.

Music – with opportunities for controlling sounds through singing and playing, performing skills, listening, and applying knowledge and understanding. The opportunity to explore music from different times and cultures arises here.

Religious Education – learning about religion, and learning from religion. There are opportunities to explore many of the themes, such as beliefs and questions, journeys of life and death, symbols and religious expression, and for visits, visitors and discussions.

Personal, Social and Health Education (PSHE) and Citizenship – The non-statutory guidelines for PSHE and Citizenship at Key Stages 1 and 2, and for PSHE at Key Stages 3 and 4, and the National Curriculum programme of study for Citizenship at Key Stages 3 and 4 provide numerous opportunities for exploring the material in this book. Issues here include looking at the role of active and informed citizens, developing good relationships and respecting differences between people, and promoting skills of enquiry, communication, participation and responsible action.

This book will also be of use to people of African and African-Caribbean descent who wish to explore their cultural roots. This can be young people themselves, parents with their children or grandchildren, or professionals working with young children of black or mixed heritage parentage who may be struggling with identity issues. Many traditions disappear with each generation or adapt to new situations and environments. Personally, in writing this book, I have experienced great joy and pride in my heritage, finding greater understanding of my parents' and grandparents' generation, and have learnt many new things.

All this has spurred me on to further research, as well as enjoying many new cooking and craft activities with my own children. Gathering the 'real life' experiences of friends and family members for many of the festivals and traditions included in this book has highlighted for me the continuance of a rich oral tradition, and a vastly untapped community resource for local and global history and culture. Have fun exploring it for yourself!

Section One

The Historical Background

People of African descent can be found living all over the world. The story of their scattering to the four corners of the globe is one of suffering – and bravery.

Although Africans had been traded across the Sahara by Arabs and Berbers since Roman times, the arrival of Europeans on the West African coast in the 1440s changed everything. By 1520, Africans were being sent in ships across the Atlantic to be slaves in the American continent.

This slave trade was the root cause of Africans' dispersal. It has been estimated that somewhere in the region of 20 million people were forcibly uprooted from their homelands in West Africa and transplanted into the hostile environment of plantations in the Caribbean and the Americas. Over the next few generations, as a result of many interacting factors, their descendants were to become dispersed all over the globe.

In keeping with their heritage, no written records were maintained by the slaves. For centuries, African cultures and traditions have been held in memory and passed down orally. In modern Senegal it is still said that when an old man dies it is as if a library has gone up in smoke. However, the down-side of this cultural trait was that people could more easily be separated from their pasts. The European owners of the plantations feared the power of the slaves if united, and so every effort was made to keep kinsmen apart to diminish the threat of uprising. Slaves from different countries, speaking different languages, were thrown together, leading naturally to a growing fusion of cultures.

Though the slaves all originated from the same continent, Africa itself was large and very diverse. What united the arrivals in the New World was their slavery, more than language or religion. Yet, remarkably, a strong African heritage endured in the Caribbean: not in the form of traditions from a particular part of Africa but rather a new hybrid creation.

Caribbean culture emerged as a patchwork composed of the remnants and influences of the myriad African peoples who were shipped across the Atlantic, and together had to create a new cultural universe. Food, dress, dance, music, stories, art, customs, languages and religions – all were transformed and adapted in response to a new environment.

This book presents this fusion of traditions, with stories from the Caribbean and from Africa – both new traditions and old. But in order to understand the nature of this complex cultural world, we must begin our journey at its source and birthplace, Africa.

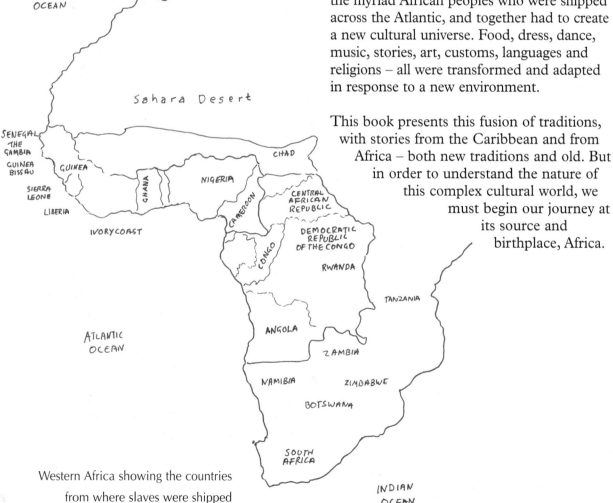

Western Africa showing the countries from where slaves were shipped

African beginnings

Most scientists now agree that Africa was the birthplace of the human race. Archaeologists have discovered tools and bones in parts of Kenya, Tanzania and Ethiopia, which date back millions of years. These early Stone Age inhabitants were hunters and gatherers, moving around in small groups, in search of food. Living this way for thousands of years, they eventually learnt how to farm, keep animals and build permanent homes.

The Iron Age brought with it the ability to clear larger areas of land for farming and the development of more specialised systems for the production of goods. People from one community began to trade with those from another, exchanging their surplus goods. The peoples from Northern and Eastern Africa moved into West Africa – originally thought to have been inhabited by pygmies – and began to settle in the area which is now the Sahara desert. At that time, the desert was a fertile savannah, which only began to dry up around 4000BC. As the Sahara dried out, trade extended across the sea of sand to North Africa. By the time of the first centuries after Christ, North African Berbers began to travel south with their camels laden with salt and copper to exchange for gold, slaves and spices.

Towns grew up along the trading routes which criss-crossed the desert. Local rulers became rich and powerful by charging taxes on the items traded, and warriors were paid to keep the peace and protect the caravan routes. Empires grew. Three of the most well-known and powerful empires to emerge were those of Ghana (based in modern Mauritania, c.700 to c.1050), Mali (based in modern Mali and Guinea, c.1150 to c.1400) and Songhai (based in modern Mali and Niger, c.1450 to c.1650).

From as early as the 10th century, the ruling, merchant and warrior classes of the empires adopted Islam as their religion, a direct result of their trading links with the Arab Berbers. Great centres of Muslim learning were established – Timbuktu being the most famous – and these provided the laws that brought order to the business of trading. Outside of such centres, in the countryside, farmers, craftsmen and miners retained more of their traditional beliefs, although these also absorbed some Islamic influences.

Ibn Battuta, an Arab traveller in the 14th century, expressed admiration for the people of Mali and the way they organised themselves. He noted their extravagant use of gold, the great respect the people had for their ruler, and stated that:

They are seldom unjust and have a greater abhorrence of injustice than any other people. Their Sultan shows no mercy to anyone guilty of the least act of it. There is complete security in the country. Neither travellers nor inhabitants in it have anything to fear from robbers or men of violence.

The wealth of the empire of Mali was confirmed to the whole world when their Emperor, Mansa Musa, made a pilgrimage to Mecca in 1324; en route, he took so much gold with him to Egypt that he caused massive devaluation in the local currency.

Later, Songhai maintained many of the same traits as Mali. In 1550, a lavish picture was painted of the city of Timbuktu under the Songhai by Leo Africanus, an African who had been born in Granada:

There you may find judges, professors and devout men, all handsomely maintained by the king, who holds scholars in much honour. There, too, they sell many hand-written North African books and more profit is made there from the sale of books than from any other branch of trade.

It is unlikely that these scholars and merchants, the inhabitants of such cities, would have been captured and taken into slavery. Many slaves would have been organised merchants or *dyula*, or would have come from farming communities who were experienced in trading their surplus food for goods. Many more slaves would have originally come from families skilled in iron and copper work, fishing or mining.

Slavery itself was not a new phenomenon in Africa; it had existed in African society before the Europeans came. However, the numbers involved were much smaller, and the way in which they were treated differed considerably from the way in which African slaves were to be treated in the Caribbean.

There were four ways in which free Africans could become enslaved in their homeland. Slaves were captured during wars between tribes or seized in raids. Others became slaves when thrown out of their tribes for committing serious crimes or breaking tribal customs. Parents could put their children into domestic slavery with a wealthy family during times of famine, to avoid them starving to death. Moreover, people could sell themselves into domestic slavery in order to pay their debts. They were then able to regain their freedom once the debt was paid.

However, all slaves were treated well, protected by the customs of the communities in which they lived. Some had the ability to earn money and buy their freedom. Others, through marriage, became members of the family who owned them, and it was even possible to rise from being a slave to the position of king. Slaves were treated as people, and retained certain rights. They could only be sold if found guilty of a serious crime.

Thus it was that when the Europeans began to arrive in the 1440s to buy slaves, there was probably a crucial gap in understanding as to what form of slavery the Africans were being sold into by their kings. The African rulers did not see it as something so terrible, but in the Caribbean slaves would be bought, sold and worked to death as if they were mere objects, not human beings.

This gap in understanding led to untold suffering, and to the fusion of American and Caribbean cultures.

New World, new culture

Originally, the Europeans had no plans for the ultimate destination of most African slaves. These early captives were taken to Europe to be slaves in the homes of the wealthy. But in 1492, a Genoese sailor named Columbus persuaded Queen Isabella of Spain to commission his voyage across the Atlantic, and a New World was discovered.

Columbus was travelling westwards in the hope of finding a way to India – to this day, many Europeans still refer to this area of the

Marriage à la Mode: IV, The Toilette by William Hogarth

world as the 'West Indies'! Even on his death, less than 10 years later, Columbus still believed himself to be in the 'East'. It took some time for this misapprehension to be corrected, and for Europeans to realise that – for them – this really was a 'new world'.

To the medieval European mind, the idea of a completely unknown continent was difficult to grasp. Some assumed the Amerindians were the lost 10 tribes of Israel. Others thought that this discovery heralded the Apocalypse, relating the discovery to the prophecy of St John in the Book of Revelation, of an old world and a new one. Drawings in the books of the age were filled with the ghoulish monsters that were assumed to be living in the Americas and the Caribbean.

The reality on the ground, though, somewhat constrained the imagination. Though gold and precious metals had originally been sought, an abundance of fertile land and an enslaved workforce that could farm the land and bring the Spanish settlers riches led to the islands of the Caribbean becoming an attractive proposition.

The friendly and trusting reception given by the indigenous peoples – the Caribs, Arawaks, Ciboneys and other Amerindian groups – was soon abused, and degenerated into open warfare, leading eventually to their subjugation. They did not fare well under the harsh treatment of the Spanish, and were practically wiped out by the fighting and the introduction of European diseases, most notably smallpox, against which they had no resistance.

By the 1600s, there were only a handful of indigenous Amerindians left in the islands, but the stranglehold of the Spanish in the area was weakening. The Dutch, English and

French began to seek influence here too. European settlers started to import poor agricultural labourers from Europe as 'bond servants' (or *engagés* in French), who were given land and tools if they survived the heat and hard labour after three or five years. However, only the very desperate were willing to leave their harsh masters in Europe for even worse conditions in the Caribbean. As the source of labour diminished, more unscrupulous methods of recruitment were adopted. Simple country folk were recruited, with no real knowledge of where they were going or of what to expect when they got there. Many drunken sailors and fishermen were 'barbodised' or seized during kidnapping raids on coastal towns. Convicts and prisoners of war were also used for labour.

Labourers recruited in this fashion were rarely treated well; many did not survive and, if they did, often did not receive the promised grant of land, sugar or small cash payment. These people, cruelly disappointed, later migrated to the new colonies in North America. Between 1650 and 1656, Oliver Cromwell sent thousands of Scottish and Irish civilians, and the remnants of armies he had defeated, to the Caribbean. However, it soon became clear that another source of labour was required.

Although the transatlantic slave trade had been 'legal' since 1519, the number of slaves crossing the Atlantic had been small compared to what took place at this point in history – when the slave trade became industrialised. Until now, the transfer of slaves had been in the hands of the Portuguese, who had a contract with the Spanish crown to supply slaves to their American colonies. But the European rivals began to fight one another for this contract, which passed to the Dutch, the French, and – finally – the English.

In Africa, too, the means used to supply slaves changed. The raiding parties of the early slave traders gave way to more elaborate forms of acquiring slaves. Pretexts for wars were found, arms were supplied to one side in return for slaves, and Africans were encouraged to capture other Africans. Well-defended trading posts grew up along the West African coast to handle the growing numbers in demand. To maximise profits, slave merchants travelled with a full cargo, usually around 450 people, and little regard for their conditions during the journey.

The middle passage

Depending on the weather and the distance to be travelled, a journey lasted anything between six weeks and three months, and approximately one in every three of the slaves might be lost through ill treatment, the insanitary conditions on board (dysentery and smallpox were common), and even suicide. Discipline was harsh, though with only around 10 sailors to every 100 slaves there were mutinies, but few were successful.

On the ships themselves, the typical amount of space allocated for a male slave was 6' long by 1'4" wide; for a female, 5' long by 1'6"; and for children 4'6" by 1' wide. It is

believed that the famous 'limbo' dance of the Caribbean originated as the only form of exercise available to slaves shackled and packed so tightly in the hold of the slave ship.

As the slaves would find when they finally reached the Caribbean, their new cultural reality was determined by these sorts of constraints.

Activity

- *Using the measurements on this page, cut out a piece of paper according to the size allocated for children and lie down on it. Imagine that this is the space you will be living in for the next three months...*

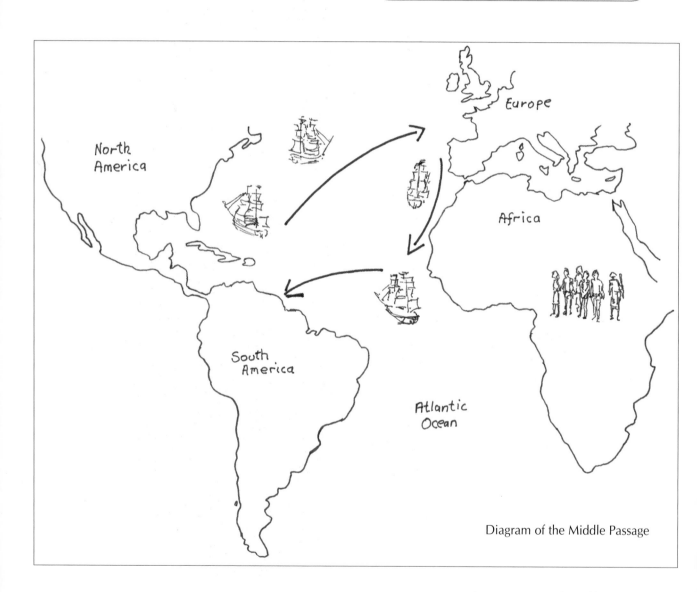

Diagram of the Middle Passage

Opposite page: Plan of boat decks showing how the slaves were packed in

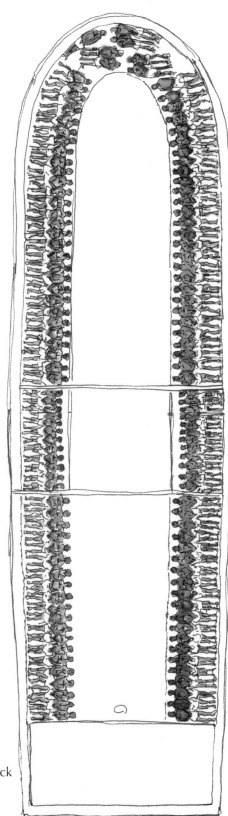

Upper deck

Lower deck

The Caribbean melting pot

The Amerindians, of course, were the original inhabitants. On some Caribbean islands small numbers of the original inhabitants still exist, despite many having mixed over the years with the variety of visitors to their shores. The influences of their predecessors can be seen today in surviving place names in the Caribbean, e.g. Jamaica from the Arawak *xaymaca*, meaning 'land of wood and water', and in items, activities and events recognised across the world, such as 'hurricane', 'canoe' and 'hammock'.

However, the cultural presence of the Amerindians is most evident in Caribbean food and its preparation – with the Arawaks being particularly significant. The word 'barbecue' and its meaning, for instance, can be traced to the Arawaks, who smoked their meat on a platform of green tree branches over a slow burning fire called a *brabacot*. One of the Arawak dietary staples was cassava, and Jamaican *bammy*, made from grated cassava, is produced today in a manner very similar to the *zabi* or *bammy* of the Arawaks. As well as food, it provided a poison used for arrows,

and to make a preservative for meat called *cassareep*, which led to invention of the seemingly everlasting 'Pepperpot Stew'. It is believed that the Amerindians kept the pot of meat and vegetables permanently (legend has it, for generations!) simmering on the fire, adding more ingredients every day, the taste of the stew improving with age. 'Pepperpot' stew (Trinidad) or soup (Jamaica) is still a favourite in many islands, though some of the ingredients such as the available types of meat and vegetables may have changed – and stews are no longer kept simmering for years!

As far as the European influence is concerned, its most obvious legacy is in language (see p.17-8 and p.115) and Christianity. The 'universal church' was crucial to slaves from the moment of their capture. Yet the Christian church was also regarded as justification for the enslavement of African peoples, who were thus granted the 'opportunity' to become Christian. In the Caribbean, the Church percolated through every stratum of settlements, and produced a heady mix of Christianity and traditional beliefs – much as Islam had mixed with traditional beliefs in Africa.

Islam

Islam was originally brought to Africa very soon after the faith arose in the early 7th century. Peoples of the new religion poured into North Africa under the leadership of the first ruler, or Caliph, Omar, and took cities such as Alexandria from the weakening Roman empire. Subsequently, as Islam strengthened its hold in North Africa, traders from this Mediterranean fringe began to look south across the Sahara to West Africa. By the early 10th century the empire of Ghana in modern Mauritania had converted to Islam, and the trading classes of the peoples on the southern fringe soon followed suit. At this time, the Islamic lands of North Africa, the Middle East and Spain were among the most sophisticated civilisations in the world. Like all empires, this Islamic world depended on trade and on slave labour, and thus, in addition to the gold which was sought in West Africa by the Muslim traders, many slaves were taken to Islamic lands – perhaps as many as were later taken across the Atlantic by Europeans. However, the forms of slavery were more varied and less brutal in the Islamic world than in the Atlantic diaspora.

Although not popular, historians acknowledge that there is much evidence in slave records and narratives to indicate that many of the slaves brought to the Americas were Muslim. This fact has even been evident in the stories of slavery that have reached television and cinema screens. Steven Spielberg's film *Amistad* features slaves who speak and understand Arabic; one of whom responds to the Islamic greeting *Assalamu alaikum* (peace be unto you) when put to the test by a missionary. Moreover, Alex Haley describes in his book *Roots: The Saga of an American Family* how its main character, Kunte Kinte was a Muslim. Historians agree that Islam has made significant contributions to Africa, particularly in the building of cities, in education and in laws of governance. Islam co-existed with African traditional religions in West Africa for hundreds of years. It has both adapted itself and adopted elements of traditional religions, until it has in some cases taken their place. Although very different on certain levels, Islam and traditional African religions share many similarities, not least by providing both a religious creed and a spiritual framework for the whole of life. In embracing Islam, then, Africans were replacing old ideas with new ones. But the old rituals, values and traditions were not completely forbidden. This sense of familiarity made conversion to Islam much easier than conversion to Christianity, especially as Islam, like traditional African cultures, endorsed men marrying more than one wife.

Linguistically too, Islam has had a major impact on Africa. Swahili and Hausa are the two most widely spoken languages in East and West Africa. Both languages have essentially evolved as languages of brokerage between different peoples, and over 1000 years of co-existing with other peoples, each has incorporated words into their vocabulary which are derived from Arabic.

About 300 million Muslims live in Africa today. The main strongholds of Islam are in North and West Africa, and especially in Guinea, Mali, Mauritania, northern Nigeria, Senegal and northern Sudan. Though in recent years, Islam has experienced mass adoption amongst Africans, this should not disguise the fact that it has an ancient presence in the continent.

A life of slavery

Following the terrible crossing of the Atlantic, slaves had to suffer the ignominy of being sold, and the terrors of life on the plantations or in the mines. As far as being sold went, in order to get the best price for their cargo captains carefully prepared their slaves for sale. They were stripped, shaved and rubbed with oil. Their sale was performed by means of either a 'slave scramble', where they were sold in groups for a set fee or later, when this was outlawed, at an auction, where they were inspected and bids were placed for them. Finally, their new master branded them.

In the Caribbean, slaves were put to work cultivating cotton, tobacco and sugar, and rearing cattle, not so much for their meat, but for the huge profits to be made from hides. Sugar soon became king of the Caribbean. In Brazil the Dutch had developed methods for making sugar production a profitable enterprise, and when they were defeated there by the Portuguese in 1654 they took this knowledge with them to other islands in the Caribbean. Sugar production considerably increased the demand for African slaves. (However, in the USA the largest number of slaves were to be

The buying of African Slaves

Pigmentocracy

(A state in which rights and resources are distributed according to the colour of a person's skin)

Negro: child of negro and negro
Mulatto: child of negro and white man
Sambo: child of mulatto and negro
Quadroon: child of mulatto woman and white man
Mustee: child of quadroon (or pure Amerindian) and white man
Mustiphini: child of mustee and white man
Quintroon: child of mustiphini and white man
Octoroon: child of quintroon and white man

Quoted in CLR James: The Black Jacobins

found on the cotton plantations, and in Belize they grew timber.) The huge profits made were brought back to Europe and were invested in large country estates and the new industries that were developing in Europe, at a period later to be called the Industrial Revolution. But whereas all this increased the wealth of Europe, the economic future of Africa was critically undermined by removal of its most important resource – its people.

Life on the plantations

Living conditions on the plantations were as horrific as the journey from Africa had been. Most plantation owners were absentee landlords who employed overseers to manage their estates. Again, the maximisation of profits was the foremost consideration. Following a period of training, known as 'seasoning', long hours from sunrise to sunset were expected from the field workers, both men and women, rising to an 18-hour day at harvest time. The only break would be for a few days at Christmas and after harvest. Pregnant women often worked throughout their pregnancy, were given a month's rest after the birth, and then were expected to

resume their duties, often with their child strapped to their back. From the age of five a child was expected to be involved in plantation work, perhaps alongside weak and elderly slaves, for example weeding or feeding the animals. Whipping and other extreme forms of punishment were commonplace and, as a result, mortality rates were high.

Domestic slaves, working in the plantation house, fared a little better and considered themselves superior to the field slave. There were also slaves with skills such as masonry and carpentry, who brought in extra income for the estate by being hired out.

Despite the long hours worked on the plantation, slaves found time to work on the small plots of land given them by law to provide food for themselves. Later colonial laws stipulated that a minimum of 26 days each in the year was to be allocated to the slaves to cultivate their own food. Their land was often many miles away from the sugar fields in the valleys, on hill slopes or in backlands. However, time and energy was found to cultivate yams, plantains, dasheens

At the top the whites:
1. *Born in Europe or in the colonies of parents of European origin.*
2. *The owners or managers of nearly all the land, nearly all the buildings, machinery, livestock and nearly all the people, who are slaves.*
3. *The only ones with political power.*
4. *Tend to decline in number as the other two groups increase. Eventually vastly outnumbered by the slaves.*
5. *Jealous of the increasing wealth of the free blacks and coloureds.*

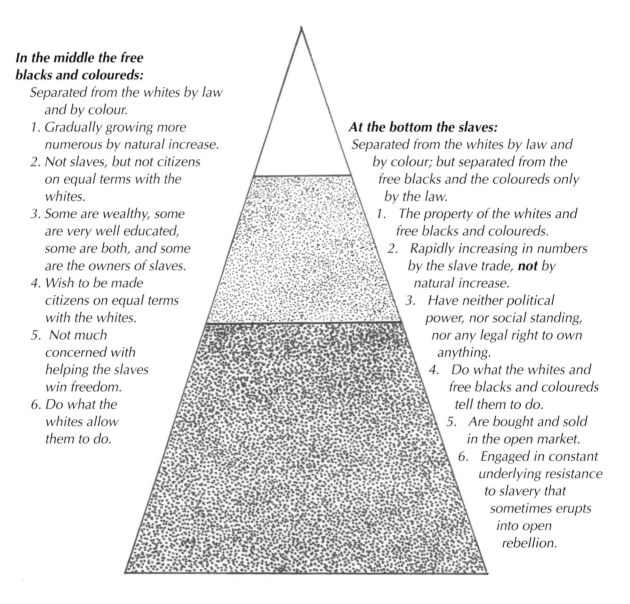

In the middle the free blacks and coloureds:

Separated from the whites by law and by colour.
1. *Gradually growing more numerous by natural increase.*
2. *Not slaves, but not citizens on equal terms with the whites.*
3. *Some are wealthy, some are very well educated, some are both, and some are the owners of slaves.*
4. *Wish to be made citizens on equal terms with the whites.*
5. *Not much concerned with helping the slaves win freedom.*
6. *Do what the whites allow them to do.*

At the bottom the slaves:

Separated from the whites by law and by colour; but separated from the free blacks and the coloureds only by the law.
1. *The property of the whites and free blacks and coloureds.*
2. *Rapidly increasing in numbers by the slave trade, **not** by natural increase.*
3. *Have neither political power, nor social standing, nor any legal right to own anything.*
4. *Do what the whites and free blacks and coloureds tell them to do.*
5. *Are bought and sold in the open market.*
6. *Engaged in constant underlying resistance to slavery that sometimes erupts into open rebellion.*

Slave plantation society

14

and other vegetables to feed themselves, and if any crops were left over, these would be taken to the local market to be sold. Female slaves gained prominence in this profession, and the *higgler* woman became an important character in the domestic economy of the Caribbean.

Resistance and heroism

Slavery was by no means simply accepted by the captured Africans. There was much resistance by the slaves during the two centuries in which slavery dominated the Caribbean. Such resistance took one of two forms. There was passive resistance: such as fooling the master by appearing simple and not to understand instructions, or by thwarting the smooth running of the plantation by damaging tools or crops, or by faking or exaggerating injuries, and therefore being unable to work. Women would prolong the process of weaning their children to delay their

return to work. Estate rules were not always adhered to, and slaves visited other plantations and were hidden by other slaves, particularly the women.

However, there is much evidence of more active and violent forms of resistance. Many slaves sought their freedom by simply running away. They were more successful in larger colonies, where they escaped to the interior and formed villages with other fugitives. They led very uncertain lives, and had to be ready to gather their belongings, but leave livestock and crops, and move very quickly if threatened by the approach of troops. However, some managed to create their own independent communities.

Life was organised in a way that combined African skills and traditions with the new skills learnt in the Caribbean. The first runaways to establish their own community were African slaves taken by the Spanish to the island of Hispaniola. They escaped to the hills and intermarried with the indigenous Arawaks. The Spanish called them Cimarrons, meaning 'those who live on the mountain top'. They constantly fought with the Spanish until a treaty was signed and they were given a large area of land as long as they handed over any new runaways. The French changed the word 'cimarron' to 'marron' and later the English called them Maroons. The English first had dealings with Maroons in the island of Jamaica, when they captured it from the Spanish in 1656. The Spanish freed their slaves, who fled to the hills to join the Maroons already established there. They became a formidable force, fighting two wars with the English, which ended with a treaty in 1739. So successful were some of these communities, that 'marronage' came to be the most important form of resistance to slavery.

Extreme measures included armed uprisings, often involving fire, and the destruction of a canefield or estate house, or slaves killing their overseer or plantation master, usually by poisoning them. Slaves sometimes even killed themselves rather than submit to the humiliation of slavery. The Igbo people (from modern Nigeria) in particular were renowned for this action on arrival in the Americas, and were branded as cowards by the Europeans. Knowledge of their culture, however, indicates the reason was most likely the fact that they were a proud people, used to self-government, and suicide was a way of expressing their resentment of the institution of slavery. Africans from the Gold Coast (modern Ghana) were generally proud and militant people, coming from a region in which there was much tribal warfare, and where courage and independence were revered. The Koromantyns were known to have bravely bared their chests for the red-hot branding iron of the slave-master,

without showing signs of pain or fear. As well as admiring them, for they were also hard-working, Europeans came to fear them. They were associated with acts of revolt, both passive and armed resistance, as in Jamaica and Guyana. Both islands had long histories of slave protest and high percentages of their slave population came from the Gold Coast (as much as 39%). Some planters later refused to take slaves captured from this region, the government of Barbados actually making it illegal for Gold Coast slaves to enter the island.

Legendary heroes emerged from the ranks of the enslaved and were added to the already wealthy store of oral history. Toussaint L'Ouverture was born a slave in the French colony of St. Domingue, and led an uprising of half a million slaves, resulting in the establishment of Haiti in 1804 – the first Black Republic in the world.

Nanny of the Maroons, who lived in the Blue Mountains in the Parish of Portland in Jamaica, led over 800 free Africans for over 50 years. A military genius, skilled in guerrilla warfare, she defended her community against attacks by the English and refused to sign a treaty with them as many other Maroons had done in 1739 and 1740. In the strong oral history of her descendants she is endowed with supernatural powers, such as keeping a cauldron boiling without any fire underneath it, catching bullets and having the ability to fly. She was from the Ashanti empire (located in modern Ghana), and her abilities equate with that of an Ashanti priest or priestess, who would advise on the best time to wage war, provide charms to protect the warriors from injury and work alongside the military leaders to perform rituals designed to weaken the enemy. She is commemorated as the first national heroine of Jamaica.

Nanny of the Maroons

It is not surprising to find a woman holding such an important position in the history of enslaved Africans. Women from the countries of West Africa were held in great esteem, especially mothers. They had authority, respect and great confidence, a heritage that ensured that they would feature strongly in the struggle to overthrow slavery. There is much evidence of slave women who showed very little respect for their masters, even singing songs that ridiculed them in their presence. They took advantage of the fact that some masters found them attractive, took them as housekeepers and common-law wives, and often fathered their children.

As domestic slaves they were the first to hear discussions at the dinner parties of their white masters, about the rights of slaves and the reform movement. This information and the work of the missionaries in the 19th century helped many female slaves to use the slave laws of the colonies and make appeals to the courts to ensure their rights were met. Although the odds weighed heavily against

them, they made their voices heard and in so doing helped to undermine the system of slavery.

Culture is what allows people to make sense of their social reality, and so, evidently, during this period of slavery, and in the midst of these unique and traumatic experiences, the spiritual and psychological needs of the slaves were met through the sharing of African traditions; of rituals, stories, riddles, dances, songs, and the playing of musical instruments. Yet inevitably, roots were put down in new lands, and adjustments made to ensure survival. New, creole cultures were created; a melting pot fusing the old from their homelands and the new from their European masters.

Language was one area in which this fusion can easily be identified. As we have seen, in an attempt to dilute the possibility of uprisings, there was a policy to separate slaves who came from the same region and spoke the same language. New languages emerged, retaining structures, words and phrases that were distinctly African in origin, from the Yoruba, Ewe, Twi and others, but greatly influenced by the languages of the European masters with whom the slaves had to converse. There are many further examples of this fusion, particularly where the African slaves were deprived of traditional aspects of their culture, and some of these will be explored in this book.

Emancipation

Slave rebellions did not make life easy for the colonists. In Jamaica, the descendants of the Maroons engaged in ambush-style campaigns against the British, and eventually secured autonomy in 1739. However, new slaves were still arriving, and were put to work on sugar plantations in the Caribbean, and tobacco and cotton plantations in the Americas. Rebellions were frequent as the slaves fought back, especially after the American War of Independence (1775-81) and the French Revolution (1789) raised hopes of the possibility of similar success, but they were crushed. The Christmas Rebellion of 1831, led by Sam Sharpe, was the last and largest of the slave revolts in Jamaica. Sharpe, who was an educated slave and a lay preacher, had advocated passive resistance, but the rebellion turned violent. Thousands of slaves went on the rampage, destroying plantations and murdering the planters. The result was that after being tricked into surrender by the promise of freedom, 400 slaves were hanged and hundreds more whipped. The campaign for the end of slavery gained strength as news of these events reached England. Although the Abolition Act of 1807 made it illegal for a British person to engage in the slave trade, trafficking continued in the Caribbean. Slavery was finally abolished on 1 August 1834 with the passing of the Emancipation Act. However, all did not go as

The Emancipation Act stipulated that:

1. *Immediate and effective measures would be taken for the abolition of slavery throughout the British colonies.*

2. *All children born after the passing of the Act, or under the age of six should be free.*

3. *All slaves over the age of six years would have to serve an apprenticeship of six years in the case of field slaves, and four years in the case of others.*

4. *Apprentices should not work for more than 45 hours per week without pay, and any additional hours were to be paid.*

5. *Apprentices should be given food and clothing by the plantation owner.*

6. *Funds should be provided for an efficient Stipendiary Magistracy, and for the moral and religious education of the ex-slaves.*

7. *Compensation in the form of a free gift of 20 million English pounds should be paid to the slave owners for the loss of their slaves.*

expected Despite being the first significant step towards freedom, for the half million slaves in the British colonies, nothing really changed for a long while.

In America, the abolition of slavery came in two stages. Many slaves gained their freedom long before Lincoln's Emancipation Proclamation of 1863, and the 13th

Amendment to the Constitution, which outlawed slavery in the United States in 1865. As the Union soldiers occupied more areas of the southern states, hundreds of thousands of slaves fled the plantations to safety within Union lines (and to join in the fight against the South) before the Confederates surrendered. The Proclamation did not apply to the whole of the US, but only to those areas under rebel control, and it helped to de-stabilise the South and allow the Union to win the war. Emancipation brought greater personal freedom, and the Reconstruction Acts of 1867 and 1868 brought basic civil rights, but a new form of racial discrimination was to give rise to a fight for equality in the 1960s.

Independence

The first Caribbean country to gain its independence was Haiti in 1804 led by Toussaint L'Overture. Haiti was followed by the Dominican Republic in 1844 and Cuba in 1902. Following World Wars One and Two, the colonial empires declined in influence and the Caribbean colonies no longer needed to fight for their independence. The British islands formed an associated federation with Great Britain in 1958, but it only lasted a few years. Jamaica, and Trinidad and Tobago, two of the then largest British colonies, left the federation first in 1962 and became independent. The federation was finally dissolved in 1966 when Barbados became independent. Guyana (formerly British Guyana) also gained its independence in 1966.

Toussaint L'Overture

Other islands followed suit in the 1970s (Bahamas 1973, Grenada 1974, Dominica 1978, St. Lucia 1979, St. Vincent and the Grenadines 1979), 1980s (Antigua and Barbuda 1981, Belize – formerly British Honduras – 1981, St. Kitts and Nevis 1983), while some remain British Dependent Territories (Cayman Islands, Turks and Caicos Islands, British Virgin Islands, Anguilla and Montserrat).

After abolition

Following the abolition of slavery across the Caribbean by the British in 1834 and finally by the Brazilians in 1888, other influences besides the European came to add their distinct flavour to the Caribbean. With the free labour of slaves no longer available, plantation owners needed to find an alternative workforce. White labourers came from all over Europe, but unaccustomed to the climate, many moved into other areas of employment or returned home. From the mid 19th century, desperation was such that the British government even went as far as recruiting labourers from Sierra Leone in West Africa to work in Jamaica, Trinidad and British Guyana. The French, Dutch and British turned to Asia and recruited Chinese and Indian immigrants as indentured

labourers. Although contracted for five years, and promised land or their return fares, these promises were rarely kept and they were forced to stay in the Caribbean. The end of the 19th century also saw an influx of Christian Lebanese (and Syrian) people fleeing the religious persecution of the Muslim Turks of the Ottoman Empire. They brought a new and rich diversity to the Caribbean in their languages, customs, food, religious festivals, music and dance.

In the days before their independence, there was also wide-scale migration from the Caribbean islands to the colonial motherlands and to America. The desire to assist in fighting wars to defend the Motherland, failing economies at home, the promise of well-paid work and education, were some of the factors at play. For a variety of reasons African traditions and customs were on the move again, destined to undergo yet more transformations – at times diluted even further, and at others strengthened by descendants keen on 'finding their roots'.

And so, the African-Caribbean diaspora which is such an integral part of today's world culture gradually took shape. This book celebrates its richness, diversity and above all its vibrant energy.

Black History Month

A people without the knowledge of their past history, origin and culture is like a tree without roots.

Marcus Mosiah Garvey

The origins of Black History Month can be found in 'Negro History Month', established in 1926 as an annual celebration in the United States of America. This honoured the contributions made in the fields of science, literature and the arts by Americans of African heritage, and took place during the second week of February. February was chosen because it was the birth month of both Frederick Douglas and Abraham Lincoln. It was officially expanded and became 'Black History Month' in 1976, during the US Bicentennial Celebration. It is widely celebrated across America with a vast range of programmes and activities.

Black History Month came into being through the efforts of Dr. Carter Godwin Goodson (1875-1950), an African-American scholar who is sometimes referred to as the 'Father of Black History'. Born the son of a former slave he missed out on a great deal of schooling through working on a farm to help support his family. Nevertheless he managed to teach himself the basics of most school subjects by the age of 17. He later moved away from home with his brother and worked as a coalminer. Eager to complete his education, he attended high school in 1895 at the age of 20, and managed to earn his diploma in less than two years. Following a few years of teaching, he became the principal of the high school in which he had achieved his diploma.

He went on to study at Berea College, Kentucky, where he gained his Bachelor of Literature degree. Following three years' work as a school supervisor in the Philippines, Goodson then travelled around Asia and Europe, studying for a while at the Sorbonne in France. In 1908 he received his M.A. from the University of Chicago, and in 1912, a Ph.D in History from Harvard University.

Goodson was horrified that Black Americans did not even feature in most history books. Where they did feature their experiences were distorted and they were depicted as inferior or sub-human. His view of history was that it should go beyond gathering facts, to include interpretation and the study of the social conditions of those particular times. So he distanced himself from mainstream academia and devoted himself to the study of the Black experience all over the world, and to creating a more balanced record.

He was the one of the founders of the Association for the Study of Negro Life and History (1915), which trained Black historians and collected, preserved and published documents about Black people and their achievements. He also founded the Journal of Black History (1916), Associated Publishers (1922) and the Negro Bulletin (1937).

Dr. Goodson hoped there would come a time when 'Negro History Week' would no longer be needed; when Americans would fully accept the contributions of Black Americans to American history. He wrote:

The achievements of the Negro, properly set forth, will crown him as a factor in early human progress and a maker of modern civilisation.

His historical research became an inspiration to generations of Black historians, and a source of dignity for Black Americans.

Black History Month – Britain

British history is a rich tapestry. But somewhere along the line a few of the threads have been pulled out. Black History Month is about ensuring that those threads are woven back into the tapestry, not left on the cutting room floor.

Trevor Philips
Chair of the Commission for Racial Equality

In Britain, Black History Month is celebrated in October. Building on the wealth of work carried out by Black British historians and communities around the country, it began in 1987 on the recommendation of the London Strategic Policy Committee (no longer in existence), as part of the 'African Jubilee Year, Marcus Garvey (1887 – 1940) Centenary Celebrations'. As with Black History Month in America, its purpose is to increase knowledge of Black history, by holding events during which this knowledge can be shared.

Events in Britain most obviously focus more on the positive contributions of African and Caribbean people to the political, economic and cultural life of Britain, although there is also great interest in the achievements of Black people in America and the rest of the world.

Black History Month has grown in prominence around the country since 1997. The Commission for Racial Equality co-ordinates a programme of events taking place during the month, and increasingly these also include contributions from British Asians. Television and radio stations, local authorities, schools, voluntary organisations and individuals, all play their part in organising events that both entertain and educate, ensuring exciting and diverse celebrations. This is a time when all communities can come together to celebrate the richness and diversity of the culture and history of Black people, but also a time for the Black community to increase its own awareness of its cultural heritage.

Activities

- *Choose a topic related to Black history and do your own research for Black History Month. Try to organise a community event and get people from your neighbourhood involved!*

Section Two

Festivals and Food

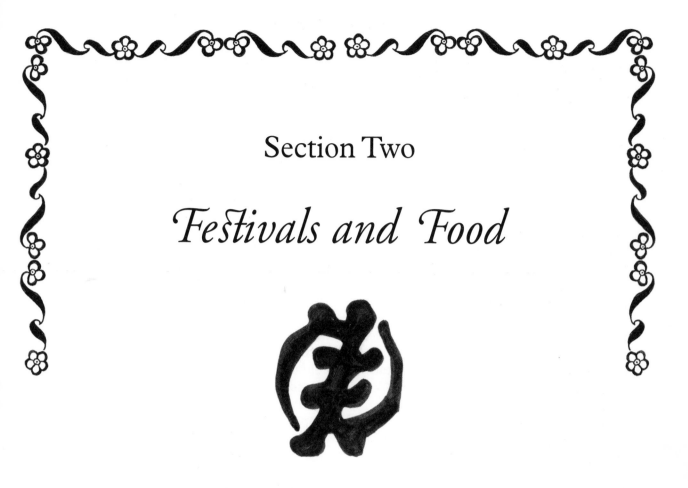

Festivals are always a time of great feasting and celebration. Most, moreover, have varying degrees of religious significance. Many festivals celebrated in Africa, the Caribbean and the southern states of North America have ancient origins, and have changed over time and adapted to new environments, as those who celebrated them moved to new areas of the world.

In keeping with the pattern of movement of African peoples from Africa to the Caribbean and the Americas, this part of the book begins by introducing several festivals from Africa, before moving across the Atlantic Ocean. Many of the festivals introduced in this section – both African and Caribbean – have their foundations in traditional African religions which view the cosmos as a combination of both visible and invisible worlds. Spirits (a supreme spirit and many lesser ones), human beings, nature and its elements are all inextricably linked, as is every aspect of sacred and secular life.

These religious beliefs have been called 'animistic' because they attribute lifelike qualities to inanimate objects, but this is a very simplistic view of what are extremely complex faiths. An all-knowing, Judaeo-Christian type of God is worshipped through the spirits and through ancestors, who mediate on the human being's behalf. Indeed, some specialists such as the Senegalese historian Cheikh Anta Diop believe that the historical origins of the Judaeo-Christian concept of God lie in Africa. Spirit possession, animal sacrifices, rituals and reverence for sacred places, people and objects are key features, and families and communities are bound together by loyalties to particular divinities and adherence to food strictures and moral prohibitions.

In the Americas, encounters with Europeans fused the traditional religions of enslaved Africans with the religions observed by the slave masters. The colonists had hoped that by isolating the different ethnic groups slaves would not be able to form meaningful associations; but the nature of their faith was found to be a common thread. While spirits and ancestors of course varied in different parts of Africa, there were many more similarities amongst the slaves' religions than between the latter and those of the slave masters.

Slaves in the Americas were therefore often forced to disguise their ancient festivals and rituals for fear of harsh punishment and even death. Enslaved Africans often took the opportunity to mock their European masters, as in the Caribbean Christmas celebration of Jonkunnu. They also adopted Christian symbols and gave Christian personalities to their tribal deities. For example in Haiti, French Catholic saints replaced the gods, or loa, and statues of saints, candles and other relics became a central part of Voodoo rites. A similar pattern occurred during early colonial history in Brazil with the cult of Santidade, where rebels against the Portuguese colonists elected their own 'popes' and 'bishops' to preach to the Indians and the slaves in the name of rebellion. These traits can be observed today with Santeria in Spanish Catholic Cuba, and Pocomania in English Protestant Jamaica.

Food plays an integral part in each of the festivals featured in this section, and – like the slaves and their traditions – it too has been transported around the world. Imported foodstuffs have been combined with local produce, prepared and cooked using both new and traditional methods, and in some cases adapted to satisfy new palates. Yams were introduced to the Caribbean from West Africa, along with recipes such as *dokono* and *fufu* (*foo-foo*), which also survived the middle passage. Many of the utensils used in food preparation such as the *yabba* (an earthenware pot in which food is cooked slowly), the *calabash* (a gourd used for storing food or water), and the *kreng kreng* (a wire basket used to slowly smoke meat over a wood fire) also came from West Africa.

Calabash

Breadfruit

Breadfruit was transplanted from Polynesia by Captain Bligh – of 'Mutiny on the Bounty' fame – to the Caribbean to become a cheap source of food for slaves. Bligh was also responsible for bringing the *ackee* tree to the Caribbean from West Africa.

Going in the opposite direction was the widely used cassava plant (*Manihot utilissima*) or *manioc*, used to make *bammy* (or *zabi*) in Jamaica, a dish originally eaten by the indigenous Arawak Indians. This is a plant native to the Caribbean and Central America, and was taken by Portuguese colonists to Africa.

Cassava is now a crucial part of African diet, from Guinea to Mozambique – its white roots, clothed in a flaky chestnut-coloured skin, can be chewed raw, and the green leaves can be cooked to make a nutritious stew. The Portuguese have played a huge role in the internationalisation of food. It is also said that the Vindaloo curries of India get their name from the Portuguese *vinha e alho* (wine and garlic).

In the most recent expression of the connections between food and African religiosity, the revolutionary cult of Rastafarianism, which has spread from Jamaica to gain importance in Britain, Canada and North America, sees food as

symbolic of the beliefs and lifestyle of the followers. Almost wholly vegetarian, Rastafarians enjoy foods in their most natural state (*I-tal* food), and have even renamed many foods. As we will see in this section of the book, this interdependency between food, festivals and belief systems is integral to the cultures of the African-Caribbean diaspora.

Cassava

Sourcing of ingredients

Although most major supermarkets now stock a range of 'exotic' fruits and vegetables, the best places to buy the ingredients needed for the recipes in this section are in the markets and high streets of towns and cities with large minority ethnic communities. African, Caribbean, Asian, and Chinese grocery stores usually stock a wide range of produce from around the world, which can generally be purchased more cheaply there.

Yam

Harvest festivals: Africa

Times of sowing and harvest have always been times of festivals and celebration in Africa, as elsewhere in the world. Though much variety can be found across the continent, most involve the offering of food as a thanksgiving, or symbol of appreciation to the gods or spirits. They invariably begin with some kind of formal religious ceremony, and end with a feast, dancing and masquerade stories telling how crops are protected by good spirits. In this way, harvest festivals are typical of the way that masquerades, dance and music often combine in events of seasonal and community importance.

First fruit festivals, celebrated by the peoples of West Africa, such as the Yoruba, Igbo and Ashanti, honour the gods for the plentiful harvest of crops by offering up the first of the crop to them. They are therefore times of great rejoicing, as they come when people are sure that hunger will not threaten.

The Yam Festival is celebrated in Ghana and Nigeria at the beginning of August, the end of the rainy season. Yam has a very special significance; it is seen as representing life and survival. Yam is the staple food of this region and is the first to be harvested. Beginning with the Feast of the New Yam, yams are prepared and offered to the gods and ancestors before they are distributed to the people of the village. The offering is made by the king or the eldest male in the community, who is then the first to eat.

The timing of the festival is also significant, as the last part of the rainy season is the time of most hunger in the seasonal cycle of West African communities. The season's end, and the harvesting of the first fruit, is thus a symbol of faith in the rebirth of the

26

community from times of hardship, and a celebration that the hardship is over.

The Nigerian writer, Chinua Achebe, gives an account of this event in his great novel, 'Things Fall Apart':

THE FEAST of the New Yam was held every year before the harvest began, to honour the earth goddess and the ancestral spirits of the clan. New yams could not be eaten until some had first been offered to these powers. Men and women, young and old, looked forward to the New Yam Festival because it began the season of plenty – the new year. On the last night before the festival, yams of the old year were all disposed of by those who still had them. The new year must begin with tasty, fresh yams and not the shrivelled and fibrous crop of the previous year. All cooking pots, calabashes and wooden bowls were thoroughly washed, especially the wooden mortar in which yam was pounded. Yam foo-foo and vegetable soup was the chief food in the celebration. So much of it was cooked that, no matter how heavily the family ate or how many friends and relatives they invited from the neighbouring villages, there was always a large quantity of food left over at the end of the day.

The Homowo Festival is a harvest festival celebrated by the Ga people of Ghana, and is the largest festival of its kind. It begins in May with the sowing of millet by priests, followed by a 30-day ban on drumming. However, different elements of the Ga tribe celebrate the festival at different times. Ga oral tradition traces the origin of the festival to when the Gas migrated and settled in Ghana, experiencing a severe famine and hardship. People worked together to survive and devised new ways of producing food in large quantities, and consequently enjoyed plentiful harvests of grain and fish. In celebration of the ending of hunger, they held a feast to jeer at hunger. The word *homowo* means 'hooting at hunger'.

The highlight of this festival is a meal made from ground corn (maize), which is steamed and mixed with palm oil, and eaten with palmnut soup.

Activities

- *Read the full account of the 'Feast of the New Yam' in 'Things Fall Apart'.*

- *Compare African harvest festivals with those that take place in your own community.*

Harvest festivals: the Caribbean

Crop Over

This is a harvest festival celebrated in Barbados, its roots firmly embedded in the harvest festival traditions of both England and West Africa. Though now much more organised across the island, the festival was initially celebrated on individual plantations or in small groups of the hundreds of sugar plantations that stretched across the island in the 1800s.

The harvesting of the sugar crop was a hard, gruelling task. Crop Over was a well-earned day of celebration to mark its end.

The proceedings began when the last load of sugarcane harvested was brought in to the mill-yard, as part of a procession of carts, pulled by animals. The cane would be bound with brightly coloured cloth and the carts decorated with flowers. In true masquerade tradition, there was much dressing up and symbolism. Leading the first cart was a splendidly dressed woman, followed by a series of characters associated with sugar production, all carrying some of the last crop of cane. 'Mr. Harding' came last. He was an effigy, dressed in trousers, coat and hat, constructed from the cane 'trash'. He symbolised the 'hard times' between sugar crops, when it was difficult to find employment.

After a few journeys around the yard, so that everyone could see the procession, there followed a little ceremony, performed with mock solemnity, involving one of the oldest

and most respected labourers and the plantation owner or manager. The labourer gave thanks on behalf of his colleagues, the owner replied and a make-shift gong proclaimed the start of the festivities.

A feast followed. Animals were slaughtered to provide meat for stews, puddings, roasts and *souse* (recipe on p.58). Rice and peas, coconut bread, *cassava pone*, fish cakes and other delicious foods were also prepared. These were washed down by a variety of beverages, both alcoholic and non-alcoholic: *swank* made from cane liquor and water, *falernum* a very sweet drink made from rum, almond and spices, and coconut water.

Music came in the form of a *Tuk* band, a group of roving musicians who played a trio of rhythms on the kettle drum, the bass drum and the penny whistle. The music was a fusion of influences from British military tradition and African rhythms, beginning slowly with a waltz, then a marching rhythm

and finally a very lively African beat. The band would be accompanied by a series of costumed characters including 'shaggy bear', 'mother Sally and 'donkey man'. Competitions such as stilt-walking, catching a greasy pig, climbing a greasy pole and 'stick-licking' kept people entertained.

Festivities ended with the burning of 'Mr. Harding', symbolising the hope that the 'hard times' that were inevitably to follow would not be too severe.

The festival disappeared in the 1940s, possibly due to the hardships encountered during World War Two. However, it was revived in the 1970s, and has been transformed from a one-day event into a national celebration running from early July, with the Opening Gala and Ceremonial Delivery of the Last Canes, to the Grand Kadooment, a costumed street parade, that takes place on the first Monday in August.

National Vodoun Day, Benin – 10 January

On 10 January 1996, President Nicephoro Soglo of Benin officially declared Vodoun a recognised religion and established a national paid holiday so that it could be celebrated. It had previously been banned by the Communist regime that had ruled the country from 1972 to 1989, and as Benin's first democratically elected President he reinstated the religion practised by more than 80% of its population.

Celebrations in the country today are marked by singing, dancing and drumming shows, and very colourful parades of marchers in elaborate costumes, most of which begin with speeches by local politicians. The national pride in something which is a central part of local culture is unmistakable.

Vodoun – anglicised as Voodoo – means 'spirit or god' in the Adja-Tado Ewe/Fon language of Togo and Benin. Anthropologists estimate that it is 6-10,000 years old, making it the world's oldest tradition of ancestor and nature worship. As well as being the official religion of Benin, it is widely practised in many parts of Togo and southwest Ghana. As many as 60 million people worldwide practise elements of this traditional religion.

Vodoun's movement around the world can be largely attributed to the slave trade. Ouidah, considered to be the birthplace of Vodoun, was one of Africa's largest slave ports. It is the home of the last surviving of five Portuguese fortresses, now a museum, which is a monument to the memory of the many who were traded into slavery from here. As a result, many of Benin's traditional beliefs can be found among people living in the Caribbean islands, especially Cuba and Haiti, in Brazil and parts of the American South.

Vodoun is more an all-encompassing way of life than a religion. Practitioners believe that all life is driven by the spiritual forces of natural phenomena in fire, wind (air/sky), earth and water, and of the dead, and that they should be honoured through rituals. Although a High God, Supreme Being or Creator, known as Mawu, is believed to have created the universe, mankind and everything that exists, his absolute power means that he is considered to be beyond the reach of humans and does not directly concern himself with them. He has delegated his powers to these spirits, the Vodoun.

Prayer is therefore not directed towards Mawu, but towards a vast array of hundreds of lesser deities who influence aspects of everyday life. Individual Vodoun communities or *cultes* are dedicated to the worship of one of these lesser gods, each of whom also has many offspring. The deities play a highly significant role in the organisation of society. Rituals are performed to initiate children and adults into their families and communities. Vodoun are woven into the poems, hymns, proverbs, artwork and oral histories of communities and provide an ethical and character-building education, based upon the tales of ancestors and heroes.

Important Vodoun spirits

Sakpata – god of the earth, and of smallpox. Feared for the terrifying nature of his power. However, he also protects against disease.

Heviosso – god of the sky and of thunder and lightning. Also responsible for the harvest, and is the symbol of justice. He punishes evil-doers.

Sakpata

Heviosso

Agbe – god of the sea, represented by a serpent, a symbol of everything that gives life.

Gu – god of iron and war.

Age – god of forests and of agriculture. He has authority over animals and birds.

Jo – god of the air, characterised by invisibility.

Legba – god of the crossroads, of unpredictability and daily tragedies.

Mami Wata – the mermaid, goddess of wealth and beauty.

Thron – a good and powerful god who protects against curses, poisons and witchcraft.

Legba

Animal sacrifices, trances brought on by spirit possession, 'vanishing acts', and the casting of spells are other features of this religion. However, followers insist on trying to balance good and evil, which is an aim far removed from the popular perception of one of the world's oldest religions. It has been characterised as superstitious, primitive, barbaric and sexually immoral. Hollywood's depiction of 'Voodoo', with an emphasis on human sacrifice, witchcraft and black magic, with cannibals, zombies, pin dolls and curses, has not helped to dispel this view. While there is no doubt that Vodoun did change on its journey to the New World, the faith of Africans survived the imposition of European religions, and was often seen as instrumental in the revolutionary struggles that ensued.

Voodoo and its branches

Voodoo – Haiti (French Catholic influence)
Santeria – Cuba (Spanish Catholic influence)
Shango – Trinidad and Tobago
Ju-ju – Bahamas
Kumina /Pocomania/ Obeah – Jamaica (English Protestant influence)
Candomble – Brazil

Eating – African style

It is widely said in West Africa that if you put an African child in front of a single, individual plate, he or she will burst into tears and be unable to eat. This is because mealtimes in Africa are always communal activities, so that everyone eats out of the same dish.

The food is arranged in a similar way whatever is being eaten. A large mound of the staple food – rice, millet, cassava – is placed at the centre of the bowl. Then the sauce – fish, perhaps, or groundnuts – is placed in a small mound at the centre of the staple. It is the host's duty to distribute the sauce in a fair and equal way to all who are eating. If there are any honoured guests, the host makes sure that they are given the choicest pieces of food. In many cultures men and women eat from separate dishes.

Food tends to be eaten with the hands, although spoons are sometimes used. In Islamic countries, the right hand is always the one used, as the left hand is used for 'unclean' practices (there is generally no toilet paper). The idea is to mash the staple into a tight ball, dip the ball in your part of the sauce, place the ball on the thumb, and then to flick it into the mouth with the forefinger so that the hand does not become covered with saliva. Novices tend to find it harder than it looks!

To Westerners, this practice seems impossible to contemplate. Used as we are to a more individualistic mode of existence, this means of eating appears frankly unappetising. In Africa, however, this communalism is an apt expression of the shared nature of life. Individual ownership forms no part in the traditional scale of values. Kinship is everything, together with respect for age.

Thus if a younger brother has something which the older brother wants, it is his duty to give it to him (in practice, of course, this tradition is itself not without its problems!). And if one member of the family has food, it is his duty to share it with everybody. In fact, anyone who is passing – family or not – when a meal is being eaten has a right to present themselves and join in. And if they are invited to eat, refusal is not an option.

This means of eating is also testament to the poverty to be found in many parts of Africa. Communalism and togetherness have tended to be practised in societies where there is little wealth: only by working together can people overcome severe lack. Thus what is lost in terms of material comfort is gained through the sense of togetherness and a shared purpose.

This philosophy imbues every aspect of life in Africa.

Recipes

Mashes and porridges are the staple of African diets. These are made from root vegetables such as yams, cassava and sweet potatoes, fruits such as green bananas, plantains and maize (sweetcorn), grains such as maize, semolina and rice, and peas and beans of many varieties. They are eaten with stews and soups.

African vegetarian stew

Ingredients:
4 small kohlrabies, peeled and cut into chunks (parsnips could be substituted)
1/2 cup couscous or bulgar wheat
1 large onion, chopped
1/4 cup raisins
2 sweet potatoes, peeled and cut into chunks
1 tsp ground coriander
1/2 tsp ground turmeric
2 courgettes, sliced thick
1/2 tsp ground cinnamon
5 fresh tomatoes, or 450g/16 oz can
1/2 tsp ground ginger
1/4 tsp ground cumin
450g/16 oz can chick peas
3 cups water

Put all the ingredients in a large saucepan. Bring to boil, lower the heat and simmer until the vegetables are tender (about 30 minutes). Serve the couscous separately if desired.

Plantains and maize

Spicy groundnut stew

Ingredients:
1 onion
5 cloves garlic, finely chopped
5 cm/2 inch ginger, cut into small pieces
4 tbsp oil
1 small white cabbage, finely chopped
3 large sweet potatoes, cut into 5 cm/2 inch cubes
1 tin tomatoes
275ml/1/2 pint pineapple juice
250g/9 oz peanut butter
350ml/2/3 pint vegetable stock
1-2 tbsp cayenne pepper (depending on how spicy you like it!)
1/2 tsp turmeric
1/2 tsp cumin
2 bananas (peeled)
2 carrots (grated)

Fry the onions, garlic and ginger in the oil, turmeric, cumin and cayenne pepper until they are soft (5–10 minutes) in a large pan. Add the sweet potatoes and cabbage, cover and cook on a low heat for 10-15 minutes, or until the sweet potatoes are soft. Add the tomatoes, the pineapple juice and the stock. Simmer on a low heat for half an hour. Add the peanut butter and stir in to thicken. Add more if need be to give a thick consistency. Top with the chopped bananas and grated carrots. The dish is best served with a side dish of yoghurt and either rice or couscous.

Many islands of the Caribbean have dishes prepared in a similar fashion. For example, the Antiguan and Barbudan National dish is Pepperpot and *fungee* (a cornmeal and okra dish). As well as being used as a part of savoury dishes, some African recipes are also used for desserts in the Caribbean. One particular dish, *dokono* (Twi for 'boiled cornbread'), has travelled from West Africa to a number of the islands of the Caribbean, and has not changed at all, in either name or ingredients, along the journey!

In his book *The Sun and the Drum: African Roots in Jamaican Folk Tradition*, Jamaican author Leonard Barrett illustrates this by telling of his childhood in Jamaica, watching his mother making *dokono* using dried corn on the cob, which she pounded into a flour in a mortar. He describes how she added sugar, nutmeg, salt and a little wheat flour to thicken it, cut it into pieces, wrapped it in banana leaves and boiled it for an hour. On a journey to Africa, to Koromantyn Market (near Koromantyn Castle, where many slaves were put on ships to the Caribbean and the Americas) he came across a woman with the same banana-tied items on her stall.

I POINTED *to it and said 'dokono'. The woman, who spoke no English, was startled. She ran and called a man who spoke English and Twi. On their way back to me, the woman was frantically explaining something to him. He finally caught up with me and asked how I knew the items were dokono. I told him that my mother used to make them and referred to them by that name in Jamaica. In a few minutes I was in the midst of a noisy admiring crowd of old men and women all talking to one another. Some came close, hugging my hands in a most caressing manner. The gentleman explained to me that the elders were giving me an African welcome because I was the son of an ancestor who was sold in slavery. He further explained that the name 'dokono' was a Fanti word which was used only among the people of the Cape Coast and that the knowledge of the name among my family was sufficient evidence that my grandparents came from the region.*

Dokono, dukunu (Blue Drawers)

Ingredients:
225g/8 oz cornmeal
110g/4 oz raw cane sugar
500ml/¾ pint coconut milk
½ tsp ground cinnamon
A few drops vanilla essence
80g/3 oz raisins

Mix the cornmeal and sugar together in a bowl. Add the coconut milk and mix until the mixture has a smooth consistency. Add the ground cinnamon, vanilla essence and raisins. Wash and 'quail' some banana leaves, by pouring hot water over them and leaving them for a few minutes until they can be folded easily. Cut the leaves into small squares. Pour the mixture into banana leaves and tie them like little parcels using the 'trash' or string. (Aluminium foil is a modern substitute for banana leaves!) Bring a pot of water to the boil and put the parcels in. Boil for an hour. Serve hot.

Cassava pone, and *conky* or *conkie* (made using sweet potato) are similar puddings, found in countries such as Belize, Barbados and Dominica. Antiguans have a dish called *ducana*, made with the all of the same ingredients, but substituting sweet potatoes for the cornmeal.

Activity
- *Make one of the above recipes and then eat a communal meal all together, African-style.*

Tabaski (Muslim feast of 'Sacrifice')

Tabaski is the largest and most important Muslim festival of the year. In the language of the Wolof people of Senegal and parts of The Gambia, the word means 'Sacrifice'.

It is a celebration in honour of the sacrifice that Abraham was willing to make of his only son, Ishmael (known as Isaac in the Judaeo-Christian tradition), when requested to do so by Allah. Abraham had been deeply troubled by the request, but nevertheless agreed to perform the sacrifice, demonstrating his absolute obedience to Allah. However, as Abraham was about to carry out the sacrifice, Allah instructed him to sacrifice a ram instead, which was caught by its horns in a nearby bush.

The festival occurs two months and ten days after the celebration of Eid al-Fitr, which marks the end of Ramadan, the month of fasting. The first day of the celebration is the 10th day of Dhul-Hijja, the last month of the Muslim year, after the end of Hajj (the pilgrimage to Mecca, performed by Muslims as one of the Five Pillars of Islam), and traditionally festivities last a few days.

The festival of Tabaski is an extraordinary time in Islamic areas of West Africa. For weeks prior to the great day, every village is witness to scores of sheep tied up near their owners' homes. People travel long distances to secure sheep at locations where they can be cheaply bought, since it is the duty of every family that can sacrifice a ram to do so. There is an atmosphere of expectation and intense spirituality. Family members must travel from wherever they are to attend if they possibly can.

On the day itself, after morning prayers at the mosque, the ram is ritually slaughtered to remember Abraham's offering. The meat is divided amongst neighbours and family members. As much as a third of the food is donated to the poor, and a great feast is prepared with the meat that remains. It is a time of prayer and celebration. Everyone wears new clothes, parents give their children presents and money, and visits are made to the homes of family and friends.

In parts of Africa, as elsewhere in the world, the festival is known as Eid al-Adha (Feast of Sacrifice) and Eid al-Kabir (The Great Feast), but in countries such as Senegal, The Gambia, Burkino Faso, Chad, Cameroon, Benin, Nigeria, Togo, and Guinea, it is known as Tabaski. In some countries it is an official government holiday. This adoption of the Wolof, and not the Arabic name for the festival is symbolic of the changes which Islam has undergone in Africa.

Activities

- *Read the version of the story of the sacrifice of Isaac in the Old Testament (Genesis, Chapter 22).*

- *Find out which are the other most important Muslim festivals.*

Roast lamb is of course the order of the day for the Tabaski meal! It is usually served with one of the staples of the West African diet: rice, cassava or *fufu*, which is made from yams.

Yam

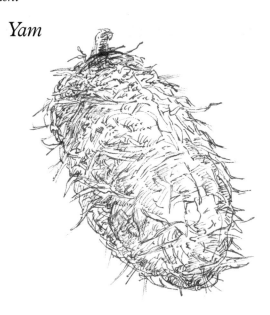

In Western and Central Africa, yam is as common as the potato is in the West; it is mashed and served to be eaten with stews and other dishes with a sauce. It is cooked in a similar fashion to potato, by boiling.

A dish called *fufu* (*foo-foo, foufou, fu fu*) forms the staple diet of many Africans. It is eaten using the right hand, which is used to tear off a small bite-sized piece, that is shaped into a ball with a hollow centre. This is then used to scoop up the stew, soup or sauce. In West Africa *fufu* is made from yams, but sometimes it is mixed with mashed plantains. In Eastern Africa (*ugali*) and Southern Africa (*sadza*) this dish is usually made with ground corn (maize), although in Uganda the staple starch is mashed plantain.

Yams are often confused with sweet potatoes, especially in the United States where the dish 'candied yams' actually consists of sweet potatoes. It is believed that the slaves in America saw the sweet potato and called it 'yam' as it was quite similar – and the name stuck! Until fairly recently, it would have been difficult to find a real yam growing in America.

The yam tuber is a starchy edible root. In the Caribbean the popular varieties include white yam (usually hard in texture), yellow yam (firm and yellow, usually used in soups), Negro yam (a soft, white yam), Chinese yam (another type of white yam) and yampie (red, white and purple varieties). It has black or brown skin which looks like tree bark, and off-white, yellow, purple or red flesh. Yams average between 1.35 kg and 3.6 kg (3 and 8lbs) in weight, but can sometimes be up to 27 kg (60lbs), and can grow to over 7 feet in length. They grow in the tropical climates of South America, Africa and the Caribbean. They were introduced to the Caribbean by the Portuguese from West Africa, where they were known by the names of *nyam*, *njam*, or *djambi*, meaning 'to eat'.

Fufu

Ingredients:
900g – 1.8kg/2-4lbs yams (white or yellow) or equal amounts of yam and plantain
Butter (optional)

Peel the skin from the yams and wash thoroughly. Cut into large chunks. Place in a large saucepan and cover with cold water. Bring to the boil and cook until the yam is soft (approximately 30 minutes). Remove from the heat and drain the water. Add butter (optional). Mash the yams, beat them and then stir until completely smooth.

(Traditionally they would be cooked in their skins.)

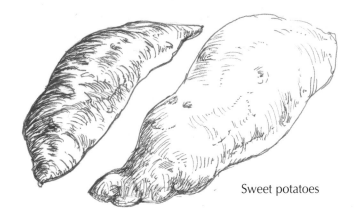
Sweet potatoes

Candied yams

Ingredients:
6 medium sweet potatoes
1/2 tsp salt
1/2 cup margarine/butter
1 cup brown sugar
1 tsp vanilla extract
1 tsp cinnamon
1 tsp nutmeg
1 cup orange juice
1 tsp lemon rind

Preheat oven to 180°C/350°F/gas mark 4. Wash sweet potatoes and parboil them in their skins in salted water for approximately 20 minutes, until fork-tender. Drain the water, remove the sweet potatoes from their skins, and cut into slices. Place slices in a greased baking dish and dot with the margarine. Make a syrup, by boiling together the sugar, orange juice, lemon rind, vanilla extract, cinnamon and nutmeg. Pour over the potatoes. Bake in the oven for about 40 minutes, basting with the syrup at intervals.

Variations:
Add chopped nuts, or miniature marshmallows before baking. Substitute a tin of crushed pineapple and the juice from the can for the orange juice.

In Ghana, yams are such an important part of the national diet that there is a yam festival. A game called Che-che-koo-lay is played by the children during the festival.

Che-che-koo-lay[1]

Here is a song from Ghana with a singing game that is played during the Yam festival.

Che-che-koo-lay, che-che- koo-lay,
Che-che Ko-fi sa, che-che Ko-fi sa,
Ko-fi sa-lan-ga, Ko-fi sa-lan-ga,
Ca-ca-shi lan-ga ca-ca-shi lan-ga,
Koom-ma-dye-day
Koom-ma-dye-day.

The children choose a child to be the leader. All of the children stand in a circle, and the leader sings the first line with hands on head; then the leader repeats it, and in the repeat (in brackets) the other children copy. The leader sings the second line with hands on shoulders; the third line with hands on hips,

and the fourth line with hands on knees. Each time, the other children copy the action as they sing the repeat. For the last line the leader falls to the ground, and the others do the same. The leader suddenly leaps up and tries to catch one of the others before they can run away. The one caught then becomes the leader.

If you play this game in a classroom, it might be better for the leader to leap up and shout out someone's name, who then becomes the leader.

Melee Ni Yaa Ee – pebble-passing game from Ghana[2]

Mele ni yaa ee
Damoshe me shebo
Mele ni yaa ee
Damoshe me shebo
Ke otay yaake manchi
Taki ake mingbi
Ke nigbe woyaa woyaa Adabraka wuamo
    gbayee.

English words by Leonora Davis:

Pass the pebble on
Try to keep it steady
Pass the pebble on
Try to keep it steady
You'll soon be out if you don't keep in time to
   the beat,
You'll soon be out if you don't keep in time to
   the beat.

Preparing for the game

After learning the song, and clapping the beat, practise tapping the floor in front of you, using your right hand, first to your left and then to the right, keeping in time to the steady beat.

Then keeping your left hand in one position (elbow slightly bent, and the hand facing upwards), clap this hand with your right hand and then tap your own right knee with your right hand (so you are still making the left to right movement with your right hand).

Next, repeat the action above, but instead of tapping your own right knee, clap the left hand of the neighbour to your right. So using your right hand, you clap your own left hand and then the left hand of your neighbour.

The game

Sit in a circle, and pass one pebble or object
around in time to the steady beat.
Next send round four pebbles or objects.
Eventually everyone has a pebble or object to
pass around the circle.

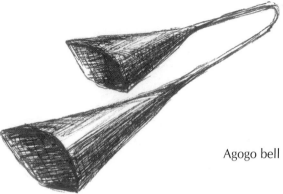

Agogo bell

Guiro

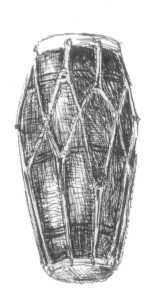

Different drums

Cassava
(Manihot utilissima/esculenta)

Cassava, or *yuca*, *manioc* or *mandioca* as it is also called, is native to the Caribbean and to Central America, but made its way to Africa with Portuguese traders from Brazil in the 16th century and later to the East. It is a tuber, with rough, veiny, brown skin, shaped like a hand with large fingers, which grows up to two feet long. Its flesh is white. There are two distinct varieties: bitter and sweet. Sweet cassava is cooked and served very similarly to potato, whereas bitter cassava, which contains poisonous prussic acid has to be cooked thoroughly before it can be used for food. Starch is extracted from cassava. In the past, the Carib Indians of the Caribbean used the starch to make bread, liquor and *cassareep*, and this still occurs today – cassareep is a liquid which preserves meat, and is the essential ingredient for Pepperpot. Moreover, the Caribs were known to use the poison to make the tips of their arrows deadly and even engaged in mass suicide by drinking cassava poison to escape enslavement by the Spanish. Besides Pepperpot, one particular dish that has

survived is the *bammy* or *zabi*, a bread made by Arawak Indians, which was eaten with fried fish. It was stored for long periods of time, and could be taken on long fishing and hunting trips without becoming stale.

Bammy
Ingredients:
450g/1lb grated cassava
1 tsp salt

Peel and grate the cassava. Place in a muslin cloth and squeeze out as much of the juice as you can. Add the salt to the cassava. Put about a cupful of the mixture into a greased frying pan. Press the mixture firmly in the pan to make a circle approximately six inches in diameter. (It is now possible to buy special bammy tins.) Place the pan over a moderate heat, and after a few minutes steam will rise. As the mixture begins to shrink, press and flatten it, and turn it over to cook the other side. Each bammy should take about 10 minutes to cook. Soak the bammy in milk, preferably coconut milk, for about 10 minutes, and fry them in oil or grill them until they are golden brown. Butter them and serve with fried fish.

Cassava

Independence days

These are times of great celebration and festivities right across the Caribbean, with demonstrations of cultural traditions in the form of music, dance and the enjoyment of traditional foods.

Jamaican Independence Day

On 6 August 1962, HRH, Princess Margaret and her husband, the Earl of Snowdon, government leaders and officials and 20,000 Jamaicans gathered in the National Stadium to witness the birth of the new nation of Jamaica. Just before midnight, the British flag was lowered, symbolically ending 307 years of British rule and the black, green and gold flag of Jamaica was raised. There was great celebration across the island with bells ringing, parties, dances and firework displays.

Jamaica now celebrates Independence Day on the first Monday in August. It has remained a day of great celebration. These celebrations have travelled to Britain, and are celebrated each year in Jamaican communities across the country with dances, dinners and cultural events.

The Jamaican National Flag

Howard Francis: Independence Then, a reflection

GROWING UP in Jamaica in the 60s as a young person was to believe that all things were possible. We were 'the baby boomers', we saw the birth of 'rock and roll', we were teenagers pushing the boundaries of parental control, we believed in the marketing dreams.

We believed that education and information would be the key to fulfilling our dreams. Jamaica was the centre of our world and in the ideal location in the Caribbean.

Although a member of the British Commonwealth our location meant that there were very strong North America and Canadian influences. So as young people we identified ourselves with the civil rights movement and Martin Luther King Jr. We easily identified ourselves with a youthful John F Kennedy when he stated in his inauguration speech 'fellow Americans don't ask what your country can do for you, but ask what can you do for your country'. And we say 'ye man' that applies to Jamaica too for we soon will be independent.

More and more of our history was being revealed, brave struggles, national heroes, and a fuller understanding of our earlier politicians and all that they had achieved to bring us to a point where we were on the brink of independence.

This was being achieved without us going to war, as so many other countries had to struggle through.

At school we had to learn our national anthem, national prayer, attend rehearsal for various activities. There was going to be activities at Kings House, soon to be the residence of our own Governor General. The Prime Minister also had a new residence 'Jamaica House'. The new House of Representatives was to be called 'Gordon House' after one of our national heroes. The Queen's representative Princess Margaret was going to be here to perform the 'handing over ceremony'.

And boy were we proud that all this was taking place at our brand-new national stadium. Our own television station Jamaica Broadcasting Corporation (JBC) was going to be up and running to broadcast live 'The Birth of the Nation' so all these new TV sets were quickly snapped up and viewing sites were set up across the island.

The scene was therefore set. We made sure we went to bed early the night before, so we would not be too tired to take in all the activities. Here we were all in our school uniforms, we were going as young people to represent the future of our new nation and witness its birth at our new stadium, but quietly we were also pleased that we were being allowed out until after midnight.

We watched all the performances, cheered and shouted as loudly as we could, we were pleased for all the young people taking part, and especially that one of the main independence messages on behalf of the young people of Jamaica was being read by Carole McGann from my own school.

Then we started to wonder what next, wishing the time away. Then at the stroke of midnight all the stadium lights went out and the spotlight picked up the Union Jack being lowered after nearly 300 years of British rule.

The spotlights then switched to the raising of the Jamaica flag of black, gold and green, and a tremendous cheer went up from the whole stadium, followed by us all singing our new National Anthem.

Congratulations abound, hugs and hand shakes were all in evidence, tears and joy all mingled together. Did the fireworks come after raising the flag and before the National Anthem or after? With the passage of time one cannot be sure.

The overall memory of that day and night will always remain strong and have a special place as the country of my birth, Jamaica.

So after 42 years what is the verdict? The power of Jamaica lies in its people. Strong, beautiful and confident we remain a force not to be taken lightly and a mystery to the unbelievers, sometimes unruly, sometimes bad, but always with love for our country.

With now nearly three million Jamaicans living overseas, what effect have we had on the world? I can say not everything is how we would like it, but we are running in the top league of the developing countries and punching above our weight in a lot of key contributions in worldwide activities and making the name Jamaica known in every country in the world.

The original Coat of Arms granted to Jamaica in 1661 was designed by the then Archbishop of Canterbury, William Sandcroft. Apart from a partial revision in 1957, it remains virtually the same as was originally designed.

The Coat of Arms shows a male and female Arawak, standing on either side of the shield which bears a red cross with five golden pineapples superimposed on it. The Crest is a Jamaican crocodile surmounting the Royal Helmet and Mantlings. The original Latin motto, 'Indus Uterque Serviet Uni', has been changed to one in English: 'Out of Many, One People'.

Produced by the Jamaica Information Service

Jamaican National Anthem

Jamaica, Land We Love, written by Hugh Braham Sherlock, and composed by Robert Charles Lightbourne, was adopted as Jamaica's National Anthem when Jamaica gained Independence in 1962.

Eternal Father, Bless our Land,
Guide us with thy mighty hand,
Keep us free from evil powers,
Be our light through countless hours,
To our leaders, great defender,
Grant true wisdom from above,
Justice, truth be ours forever,
Jamaica, land we love,
Jamaica, Jamaica, Jamaica, land we love

The Jamaican National Bird, the Doctor Bird or Swallow-Tail Humming Bird. This bird, with its iridescent feathers, has been immortalised in Jamaican folklore and song

Teach us true respect for all,
Stir response to duty's call,
Strengthen us the weak to cherish,
Give us vision lest we perish,
Knowledge send us Heavenly Father,
Grant true wisdom from above,
Justice, truth be ours forever,
Jamaica, land we love,
Jamaica, Jamaica, Jamaica, land we love.

Food is – of course! – a central part of the independence celebrations, and in Jamaica it comes in varied and delicious forms, from roast breadfruit to a mixture of Ackee and Saltfish, and delicious desserts known as *gizadas*. The recipes for these are an essential part of Jamaican cuisine.

Breadfruit

The breadfruit tree (*Artocarpus communis*) is a member of the fig family and is believed to have originated in Java (Indonesia). It is one of the tallest trees in the tropical rainforest, reaching a height of 80 feet. An individual breadfruit, large, round and green in colour, with dimpled skin, can weigh up to 4.5kg.

The breadfruit, or *ulu*, is native to Polynesia, and was brought to Jamaica by the English Captain, William Bligh, of 'The Mutiny on the Bounty' fame. News had reached Britain in the 18th century of the nutritious qualities of this remarkable plant, which produced super-strong islanders. It was hoped that it could be transported to become 'fuel' for the slaves of the British West Indies. An expedition was mounted in 1787. It failed. Captain Bligh set sail in the Bounty to Tahiti and gathered 1,000 *ulu* shoots to take to the Caribbean. However, the young plants needed plenty of water and soon had more than their fair share of the precious supply of drinking water on board ship. Bligh rationed the water for the crew and when things became too bad, they took control of the ship and put him, his supporters and the 'precious' cargo adrift. However, Bligh survived to make another attempt and on 5 February 1793 he arrived from Tahiti on HMS Providence with 347 trees. Ironically, the slaves did not take to a diet of breadfruit. It was only after the abolition of slavery that the breadfruit became popular in the Caribbean.

Roasted breadfruit

Ingredients:
1 breadfruit

Pierce the skin in several places and cook whole over a charcoal grill, or in the hot embers of a wood fire. It can also be cooked in a traditional oven. Turn the fruit regularly as the skin begins to char. It should take 45-60 minutes to roast. Steam will begin to escape from the stem end.

The charred skin can then be peeled off, the heart discarded and the flesh or 'meat' sliced and served. Delicious with butter!

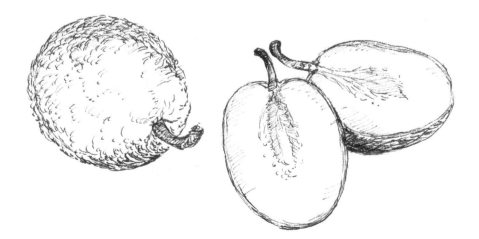

Breadfruit

47

Ackee (Blighis sapida)

Though part of Ackee and Saltfish, the national dish of Jamaica, the *ackee* tree is not native to the Caribbean. Plants were brought across the Atlantic on a slave ship from West Africa in 1778. Its name is derived from the original name *Akye fufo*, which is from the Twi language of Ghana. The tree is an evergreen, growing up to 15m/50 feet in height and bearing fruit twice a year, January to March and June to August. It has glossy green leaves and its pear-shaped red and yellow fruit (approximately 7.5–10cm/3-4 inches long) grow in bunches. The fruit turns red when ripe and the pods split open under continued exposure to the sun, displaying three large shiny black seeds, each attached to yellow flesh (aril) – the edible (and important!) part. It is at this point that the food is harvested, the aril cleaned and the red fibre and black seeds removed before it is prepared for cooking. The water that it is cooked in must be thrown away. Eating unripe *ackee* can be very dangerous, and has in the past led to fatalities.

Ackee is now canned in Jamaica and exported across the world. In Britain it can be purchased from the shelves of most Caribbean and Asian grocery stores, and even some supermarket chains. It is served in Ackee and Saltfish or for breakfast or as a starter.

It is also the subject of a popular traditional folk song, 'Linstead Market'. Here are a few of the verses:[3]

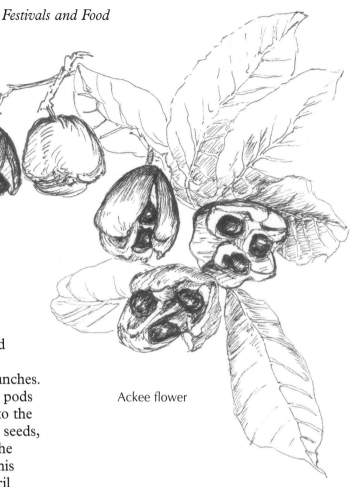

Ackee flower

Mi carry mi ackee go a Linstead Market
Not a quattie wut sell
Mi Carry me ackee go a Linstead Market
Not a quattie wut sell

Lawd what a night, not a bite
What a Saturday night
Lawd what a night not a bite
What a Saturday night

Everybody come feel up, feel up
Not a quattie wut sell
Everybody come feel up, feel up
Not a quattie wut sell

Lawd what a night, not a bite
What a Saturday night
Lawd what a night not a bite
What a Saturday night

Jamaican National Dish: Ackee and Saltfish

Ackee and Saltfish

Ingredients:
450g/1lb saltfish (preferably cod)
1 tin ackee
110g/4oz margarine or butter
Few rashers of bacon (or salted pork), cut
    into strips (optional)
1 large onion, cut crosswise in circles
2 spring onions
Sweet peppers (red, yellow and green), cut
    crosswise in circles
2 tomatoes, chopped
Thyme
Black pepper
Salt
Scotch bonnet pepper (optional)

**Note: Scotch bonnets are among the
    hottest peppers in the world, and it is
    best to wear gloves to handle them.
    Even the smallest drop of pepper
    juice can cause incredible pain if
    rubbed in the eye.**

Soak the fish overnight to remove the salt, or
boil for about 15 minutes. Drain and rinse.
Remove the skin and bones from the fish and
flake the flesh. Melt the margarine/butter in a
frying pan and fry the bacon strips for a few
minutes, adding the onions, peppers,
tomatoes and thyme. Cook gently for about
5 minutes and then add the fish. Season with
salt and black pepper. Cook for 10 minutes.
Open the tin of ackee and drain. Add
contents and very gently stir in. Cook for
about 5 minutes. Serve with any or all of the
following: rice and peas, yam, green bananas,
sweet potatoes, dumplings (fried or boiled)
and roast breadfruit.

Gizadas

These are coconut-filled pastry tartlets, with crimped edges, also known as 'pinch-me-rounds'.

Ingredients:
225g/8 oz shortcrust pastry
The grated flesh from half a small coconut
80g/3 oz cup demerara sugar
½ tsp cinnamon
½ tsp ground ginger
½ tsp grated nutmeg
3 tbsp water

Heat the oven to 200°C/400°F/gas mark 6. Mix all the ingredients except the pastry together in a small saucepan, then stir in the water. Cook gently over a low heat, stirring constantly, for about 5 minutes. Leave to cool. Roll out the pastry, cut small circles and crimp the edges with your thumb and forefinger, so that they form a ridge all the way round. Spoon some of the coconut mixture into each one. Bake for about 20 minutes, or until the pastry is golden and the coconut filling turns brown.

Delicious!

Gizadas/pinch-me-rounds

Escoveitch/Escovitch fish

Variations of this dish are found in many Latin American countries. It originated in southern Spain, where it was called *escabeche*, and comes from the word meaning 'to pickle', an early method for preserving food. In Chile and Peru it is known today as *ceviche*, and is one of the national dishes.

Ingredients:
1kg/2lb fresh snapper, jackfish (or any fish)
Lime juice
Salt
Black pepper
Cooking oil

Pickle:
Onions
Cho chos (small, oval, slightly indented green vegetables – the nearest vegetable in terms of taste and texture is a marrow)
Scotch bonnet pepper (to taste)
Pimento berries
1 cup vinegar

Note: Scotch bonnets are among the hottest peppers in the world, and it is best to wear gloves to handle them. Even the smallest drop of pepper juice can cause incredible pain if rubbed in the eye.

Wash the fish, rub them with the lime juice and dry them. Season them with salt and pepper. Heat plenty of oil slowly, until very hot and beginning to smoke. Place the fish in the oil, reduce the heat and fry on both sides until golden brown. Drain the oil from the fish and place in a dish. Peel the cho chos and cut them into long strips. Slice the onions. Put the cho chos and onions in a saucepan with the peppers, pimento and vinegar. Add a little salt to taste. Bring the mixture to the boil and simmer for a few minutes. Pour the pickle mixture over the fish. Serve, hot or cold, with bammies, hard-dough bread or Johnny cakes.

This dish will keep for up to 3 days and can be left to marinate, but some people prefer to eat it hot, while the vegetables are still quite crisp.

Sweet peppers and carrots, cut into strips or sliced, are often now added to this recipe in Britain to give it colour.

Christmas

Christianity is widespread in the Caribbean, as it is all over the world. However, Christmas in the Caribbean is a particularly magical time, when peoples of all the religions represented take part in the festivities. Many of the traditions and foods surrounding the celebration of the Christian festival of Christmas in Europe are evident in the Caribbean, but have been adapted to incorporate locally grown foodstuffs and cultural traditions.

Christmas cards are sent to friends and relatives both at home and all over the world. Since colonial times, these have been imported from England and America. But in the past they did not, as now, depict typically Caribbean scenes. Images of a 'White Christmas' have now gone, and have been replaced with pictures of more appropriate climatic conditions and scenes, such as sunshine and masquerades, and with words also reflecting the realities of a Caribbean Christmas.

Moreover, the advent of technology has enabled families and friends to keep in touch via the telephone and internet. It is common for local radio stations in the Caribbean to record telephone greetings from relatives living overseas and to broadcast them live on Christmas Day.

As elsewhere in the world, the giving and receiving of gifts is central to the Caribbean Christmas. These are either sent or taken and handed to friends, relatives, work associates or needy people in the locality. Again, as elsewhere, it is a particularly joyful time for children who traditionally receive new clothes, toys and games. Gifts are brought to them by figures representing variations on the theme of Santa Claus or Father Christmas, who along with his helpers travels from the North Pole on Christmas Eve, to deliver gifts to worthy children.

In Haiti, *Papa Noel* leaves Christmas gifts in and around childrens' scrupulously cleaned shoes, which are left, filled with straw, under the Christmas tree or out on the porch. Suriname has *Goedoe Pa* (Dearest Daddy) and his servants, for whom children leave out cookies and milk as refreshments. *Goedoe Pa* also leaves gifts, with poems attached, next to childrens' shoes. However, he and his helpers arrive much earlier, on the morning of 6 December. Interestingly, they are all black men. However, in the days before 1975, when Suriname was a colony of the Netherlands, these gifts were delivered by St. Nicholas (*Sinterklaas*), an old white man, who arrived by ship on 5 December, the day before his birthday, on a white horse with his black servants. Children left hay and carrots in their shoes for his horse to eat. Christmas Day, 25 December, and the day after, which they call *Tweede Kertsdag*, are national holidays, and are celebrated with gifts, parties and traditional foods.

Unlike at present, with Christmas lights and decorations imported from the United States and Britain, homes in the Caribbean were traditionally redecorated in time for Christmas. New furniture was purchased, or old furniture was given a new coat of varnish and polished in time for the big day. Christmas Eve was a time of busy preparation. In some islands, Christmas trees or pine branches are decorated, and nativity scenes are put together and placed beneath the tree.

Church services, and Midnight Mass in Catholic territories, play an important part in the celebrations, as does a wide array of music from carols, religious and folk music to carnival and *parang*. In Grenada, *parang* groups travel from house to house, serenading, and in Carriacou, a dependency of Grenada, there is an annual Parang Festival held on the weekend before Christmas. Christmas in St. Vincent begins on 16 December, with the start of 'Nine Mornings', running for nine days to 24 December. A tradition unique to the island, there is music, singing and celebration starting each day at 4am.

Of course, Christmas would not be Christmas without feasting! Traditional Christmas fare varies from island to island, and is as varied as the original traditions of the peoples who live there.

In Antigua, it is traditional to eat pork at Christmas, which is either baked, stewed or corned (preserved in salt or brine). Pepperpot, a slowly simmered stew of meat and vegetables (most notably pork, spinach and okra) is served on Boxing Day. However, the celebration of Boxing Day as a public holiday is alien to the many islands of the Caribbean and to the United States. A Bank Holiday in Britain, it is celebrated in areas that were colonised by the British. The origin of Boxing Day is supposedly the custom of boxed Christmas gifts that were given to workers by their employers.

In Barbados, food on offer includes baked ham, yam pie, candied sweet potatoes, plantains, *conkies* or *dunkanoo* (recipe on p.35), *jug-jug* (a stew of guinea corn, pigeon peas, salted beef and pork), and green peas and rice. Plum, or Christmas Pudding, Christmas cake (recipe on p.58) and *cassava pone* are served as desserts.

The traditional Christmas food of Guyana consists of garlic pork, pepperpot, ham, pickled onions, black cake, ginger beer, sorrel, *mauby* (a drink made from soaking the bark of the *mauby* tree and mixed with aniseed, cinnamon, angostura bitters and sugar, and also consumed in Barbados and Trinidad and Tobago), and sweet potato fly (a fermented drink).

Haitians of all ages drink a mildly alcoholic drink called *anisette*, which is made from soaking the leaves of the anise plant (of which aniseed is the seed), adding a little rum and sweetening with sugar. *Reveillon* (from the French verb 'to wake up') is a meal which begins in the early hours of Christmas morning and lasts until almost dawn.

The inhabitants of Montserrat, which was established as an Irish-Catholic colony, enjoy roast pig, goat water, a stew consisting of goat meat, spiced with cloves, rum and *herbs and chibble* (thyme and scallion), and potato pudding and *dunkanoo* (Blue Drawers in Jamaica, recipe on p.35).

In Trinidad, stewed pigeon peas and *pastelles* – small cornmeal parcels filled with a mixture consisting of meat, olives, capers and raisins which are steamed in banana leaves – are served. A delicious type of rum-laced egg-nog, called *ponche de crème*, is also consumed.

Christmas in Cuba

Christmas in Cuba before the Communist revolution of 1959, which brought Fidel Castro to power, was similar to that celebrated in Spain.

Noche Buena (Good Night) was celebrated on Christmas Eve. Extended families gathered and would feast and dance. Whole pigs were roasted in backyard pits, over coals, and covered with banana leaves, and later marinated with *mojito*. Yuca (also known as tapioca, manios and cassava elewhere in the Caribbean), fried mashed plantains, mixed salads, and rice and black beans (known as *Moros y Cristianos* – Moors and Christians). Black beans and white rice, a reminder of the medieval wars between the darker-coloured Muslims and the whiter Christians in Spain, were traditional accompaniments. Festivities would end with everyone attending Midnight Mass together. Christmas Day would be quiet, and gifts would not be exchanged until Epiphany (6 January). Children were told that these were brought by the *Reyes Magos* (magi). Traditions such as Christmas trees were introduced to Cuba from the United States, and by the 1950s Christmas was very commercialised with, among other things, Santa Claus bringing candy (sweets).

In 1962 Cuba became an officially atheist country. Christmas celebrations were allowed to continue until 1969, when Cubans were told that it was necessary to increase the productivity at sugar-harvest time (which began on 26 December). This ban on religion remained in force until 1997 when, in honour of the historic visit of Pope John Paul II to Cuba in January 1998, President Castro declared Christmas an official government holiday. Catholics in Cuba now attend Midnight Mass, church bells ring to herald the start of Christmas Day and traditional celebrations have been resumed.

Turkey

I wish the Bald Eagle had not been chosen as the representative of our country; he is a Bird of bad moral character; like those among men who live by Sharping and Robbing, he is generally poor and very lousy. The Turkey is a much more respectable Bird, and withal a true original native of North America.'

Benjamin Franklin

When the Founding Fathers were engaged in the task of choosing a bird to represent their new nation, Benjamin Franklin made it clear that the Turkey was his favourite candidate. It was later to become a symbol of the American day of Thanksgiving, as well as Christmas around the world.

The wild turkey is native to northern Mexico and the eastern USA. Fossil evidence shows that it had been around for millions of years. Native American Indians made use of them for both their food value and their feathers, which were used for decorating clothing and ceremonial articles, as well as for stabilising the arrow in flight. To some tribes it is considered sacred. The Navajo have a myth that says that their knowledge of corn and its cultivation comes from the turkey.

There are many suppositions in existence as to where the turkey got its name. One idea relates to Christopher Columbus who, thinking he was in India, called it a *tuka*, which is the Tamil word for peacock. Another attributes it to the mispronunciation of a Native American word for bird, *firkee*. Yet another theory believes the name resulted from the Spanish bringing it back to Europe, where it very quickly gained popularity in countries such as England, France and Italy. The English apparently called them turkeys after mistaking them for the West African guinea fowl, which came to England via merchants from areas in the Turkish Empire, and which they called the 'Turkey Bird' or 'Turkey-Cock'. Or... it may have simply derived from the sound a scared turkey makes – 'turk, turk'.

Paul Mathurin: Christmas in St. Lucia

M Y MEMORIES of Christmas in St. Lucia are a combination of those from my early childhood growing up on the island and those gleaned from many visits over the years to St. Lucia at Christmas time. As St. Lucia is a predominantly Roman Catholic society, many of the traditions are of that religion. The two largest celebrations on the religious calendar were Easter and Christmas and it seemed as if thoughts turned to Christmas as soon as Easter was over.

Everyone looked forward to Christmas. All the family would be involved in the preparations. The house would be cleaned, both inside and out, with the children given the responsibility for cleaning up the front yard and taking up the weeds. Children would get new clothes. We would have a Christmas tree, which we would decorate with tinsel and hand-made paper streamers. There were no Christmas tree lights like we have now, or store-bought tree decorations. Our parents would buy the paper and we would use scissors to cut out different shapes, and we would decorate the whole house with these too. My mum would write wads of Christmas cards to send to neighbours and relatives, those on the island and those overseas.

The preparation of food and drink would also begin months in advance. Now, many people drink alcohol, but when I was a child I remember drinking sorrel, ginger beer and drinks made from fresh fruits such as soursop and passion-fruit. Sorrel was prepared over a long period, not as quickly as it is now. About a month before, the buds would be picked, boiled, put to soak and left to almost ferment. We would also have a fruit cake, with dried fruit such as prunes, raisins and currants which were minced and soaked in wine. More affluent families would soak the currants in spirits such as brandy.

If neighbours had sheep or roosters, they would kill them and the meat would be shared in the community; sometimes paid for, or exchanged for produce. Some people had turkey, others chicken and pork joints. But Christmas would not be Christmas in St. Lucia without a salted ham! We looked forward to it. St. Lucia imported the ham from countries such as Trinidad and Venezuela. We had to order it. I still carry on that tradition with my children here in England at Christmas. It was boiled with onions, to give it more flavour, and cooked very slowly. Then cloves were put around it to give added taste. We also ate different yams that were available according to the season. I remember soft white yams and yellow yams, which had French names, because ours is a French-influenced island. We also had macaroni and cheese, rice with a side dish of stewed peas (red beans) or pigeon peas. The food was cooked in great quantities, as it would last for the whole of the festive period.

Sorrel

Sorrel, also known as *roselle* in parts of the Caribbean, is a member of the Hibiscus family and native to tropical Asia. The leaves or petals are peeled off the seeds, often after it has been dried in the sun, and used to make wine, jam, drinks and a jelly. Sorrel is traditionally the favourite drink for Christmas and the New Year in many parts of the Caribbean.

Sorrel

Ingredients:
8 cups sorrel petals
50g/2oz grated ginger
12 cups boiling water
rum
sugar

Place the sorrel and ginger in a large container and pour on the boiling water. Cover and leave overnight, then strain through a muslin cloth or sieve. Add a little rum to preserve and sugar to sweeten. Bottle and refrigerate. Makes approximately 2.75 litres/4½ pints.

Souse

Also known as 'pickled pork', this dish is a delicacy enjoyed at Christmas in a number of Caribbean islands, such as Trinidad and Tobago, St. Lucia and the Bahamas.

Ingredients:
Young pig's head
4 pig's trotters (or 1.4 kg/3lbs pork meat)
4 large limes, squeezed
Salt to taste
1 medium onion, finely chopped
1 large cucumber, peeled and thinly sliced
2 scotch bonnet peppers, de-seeded and
    finely chopped
Parsley

Wash the pork well, place in a large saucepan of boiling water and simmer gently until tender. Remove from the saucepan and cool the meat in cold water. When cool, cut the meat into bite-sized pieces. Make about 2 cups of brine with the lime juice, salt and water; add the onion, cucumber and peppers, and pour this over the meat. Cover and place in the refrigerator to chill for several hours. Garnish with parsley before serving.

Note: Scotch bonnets are among the hottest peppers in the world, and it is best to wear gloves to handle them. Even the smallest drop of pepper juice can cause incredible pain if rubbed in the eye.

Black Christmas cake

This very rich cake is eaten at Christmas, weddings and other special occasions. It is known as Black Cake because traditionally the recipe uses burnt sugar. It is prepared many months in advance, as the currants and raisins have to be ground, stored in glass jars and soaked in rum for curing, and often portions of the cake are posted to relatives overseas in time for Christmas. A variation is found in many islands of the Caribbean.

Ingredients:
500g/1lb 2 oz mixed fruit
50g/2 oz cherries
100g/4 oz prunes, stoned
½ bottle of fruity red wine or ruby sherry
    (fruit must be prepared in advance)
1 lime, rind and juice
1 lemon, rind and juice
900g/2lb dark, soft brown sugar
1 tbsp golden syrup
1kg/2lb 3 oz softened butter
16 eggs, beaten
2 kg/4lb 4 oz self-raising flour
100g/4 oz ground almonds
½ tsp salt
3 tbsp gravy browning (for colour)
2 tsp brandy essence
2 tsp rum essence
2 tsp sherry essence
3 tsp almond essence
3 tsp vanilla essence
2 tsp nutmeg
2 tsp cinnamon
2 tsp ground mace

Use one deep 12-inch round cake tin or two 10-inch round cake tins.

Wash the mixed fruit and prunes, pat dry. Place them and the cherries in a food processor and process until finely chopped. Add the wine/sherry. Transfer to a large clean jar and cover with a lid. Leave to soak for a few weeks – the longer, the better the flavour will be. Stir the fruit mixture occasionally and keep covered, adding more alcohol, if you like.

Preheat the oven to 170°C/325°F/gas mark 3. Grease and line 2 round 25 cm/10 inch cake tins with a double layer of greaseproof paper. Cream together the butter and the sugar. Remove 'eyes' from the eggs, and whisk gently. Add the eggs slowly until the mixture is smooth and creamy. Add the gravy browning, fruit mixture, almonds, essences, spices and golden syrup. Grate the rind from the lemon and lime, add to the mixture. Squeeze the juice from them and add also. Add salt to the sifted flour, and fold in to the mixture. The mixture should not be too stiff or runny; it should just fall off the back of the spoon. Spoon the mixture into the prepared tin, and bake for about 3½ hours until the cake is firm and springy. Test with a skewer, which should be clean when removed if the cake is cooked. Leave to cool in the tin. Sprinkle the cake with more rum if it is not to be used immediately. Wrap the cake in greaseproof paper and foil to keep it moist.

This cake can also be frozen for use at a later date.

Jonkunnu (John Canoe, Junkanoo or Jonkunoo)

Jonkunnu is an essential festival in many areas of the Caribbean. In some cases, people spend virtually the entire year preparing their costumes and saving up for the big day, when the almighty carnival takes centre stage. The most traditional bands consist of a Cowhead or Horsehead, a King, a Queen with a veil, a Devil, and 'Pitchy-Patchy' dressed in tatters and rags, performing acrobatics; but over the years many more characters have been added, from both African and Caribbean influences. Spectators can be heard to cry 'Jonkunnu a come!' and the excitement brings people from their homes to line the streets to enjoy the entertainment.

Everyone, children and adults alike, participate in the festivities, running from the Devil brandishing his pitchfork, or the Cowhead, attempting to butt anyone found in his path. Musicians accompany the procession, playing a rhythm in 2/4 or 4/4 time, with a fife or flute, drums and rattles featuring prominently. Whistles are often blown by the leader of the troupe, cowbells clanked and horns are sounded. In the days of slavery, the *gumbay* drums (Jamaica), banjo and grater would also have featured. Although there is much variation, men usually play all of the characters, wearing mesh masks (with faces painted on them), wigs and other miscellaneous accessories for the female characters. Each character has a special role to play and often a special dance all of their own. There is little (whispered) or no speech, as identities are supposed to remain unknown. Spectators are expected to give donations towards the costs of the band and to provide refreshments for the entertainers.

As with all customs and traditions, Jonkunnu was affected by historical events and cultural influences. At first slaves were encouraged to hold the festival by the slave masters who actively promoted it on their plantations, but later they discouraged it when there were fears of slave uprisings. European elements were absorbed in the form of the slaves imitating their masters, evident in the music and dance steps, e.g. jigs, polkas and reels. Morris dancing and English mummery were also identifiable as influences. Later, French-Creole Carnival celebrations also became fused with Jonkunnu (see p.116).

Right up until the 1950s and 1960s in Jamaica, masked Jonkunnu bands could be seen at Christmas time all across the country, playing music, dancing and generally entertaining folk. Today it is mainly a form of entertainment at cultural events. However, Jonkunnu is still celebrated in many parts of the Caribbean that were British possessions, and is very much a major event in the Bahamas, Belize, St. Vincent and North Carolina in the USA.

The exact origins of Jonkunnu are unknown and, over the years, it has been the source of much research and scholarly debate. Of the many explanations put forward, the most plausible is that to be found in Frederic Cassidy's book, *Dictionary of Jamaican English*. He proposes that the word Jonkunnu originates from words in the Ewe language of Eastern Ghana and Togo, which sound similar: *dzono*, meaning sorcerer, *kunu*, meaning deadly, and *nu*, meaning man. Elements of Jonkunnu – e.g. the music, dance, characters, masquerade and secrecy – have also been used as the basis of a plausible explanation that these had their origins in West African secret societies, especially common in areas of modern Sierra

Leone. The earliest masqueraders were definitely associated with fear and secrecy, and these key elements have been maintained where the custom is still practised.

Another possible origin is that the festival is connected with a character by the name of John Connu or Conny. Sources show him to have been a very wealthy West African leader, who ran the Brandenburg African Company trading fort on the Gold Coast. This might have some truth, as records show that the British preferred their slaves to come from the Ashanti people of the Gold Coast, and the term Jonkunnu occurs more in former British territories of the Caribbean. It would also account for the fear associated with the character, portrayed through a grotesque mask.

Another theory links it with West African yam and harvest festivals. These involved masked dancers, who represented ancestral spirits, magnificent costumes and processions. The prominent use of animal symbolism in masks, and stilt-walkers, also support this theory.

A more contemporary definition places some relevance on the use of the word 'junk', and most definitely the use of unwanted materials has been integral in the making of costumes and instruments. For example, the *goombay* drum (Bahamas) is constructed from a metal or wooden barrel that might have contained food, rum or oil, with a sheep or goat skin stretched over one end, and decorated with geometric patterns, fragments of glass and bottle tops.

One conclusion is that Jonkunnu is a creation of the slaves in the Caribbean. From Emancipation in 1838, it began to decline as a celebration. Some would say that, just like Anansi and Brer Rabbit, Jonkunnu was a symbolic form of self-expression to outface the powerlessness of their enslavement; an act of rebellion. Christmas was obviously a grand occasion for the planters and slave-owners, and it is not surprising that they allowed the slaves a little time off. Most slaves were generally given only three days' holiday per year: Christmas Day, Boxing Day and New Year's Day. (However, slaves held by Jews in the Caribbean were given the Jewish sabbath off.) Boxing Day was given over to Jonkunnu dancing, which took the form of a masquerade through the town or village, entertaining both their masters in the plantation house and their peers in the slave houses. Escaping from the drudgery of their work of the rest of the year, they would dress in finery and enjoy themselves. They would enter a world of make-believe, giving themselves important English names, and were allowed a little more freedom by their masters.

Whatever the truth of its origins, Jonkunnu is a great show, a celebration of triumph over adversity, and testament to the enduring importance of African origins in the diaspora.

Principal Jonkunnu characters

Pitchy Patchy

Probably the most popular of all the characters. His outfit consists of strips of very colourful materials, sewn together in tiers, and a hat, either a square or a feathered cap, decorated with mirrors and tinsel. He performs acrobatics, leaping, twirling and running in and out of the midst of the crowds, growling at them. The exact origins of this character are not known. Over the years, he has been many things to many people. Oral tradition, however, connects his costume with that worn as camouflage by the Maroons, during their wars against the British.

Devil

The Devil is usually dressed completely in black, although there are sometimes red decorations. He carries a pitchfork and has a cowbell fastened to his bottom. He wears a conical-shaped cardboard headdress decorated with mirrors. It is interesting to note that people run from him in the procession – in some circumcision ceremonies in West Africa, there is a figure known as the *kankoran* from whom people also flee when he appears.

Horsehead

A painted skull of a horse, complete with eyes and a moving jaw, is fixed on a pole, which has a piece of cloth draped around it for the body. His prop is usually a whip. He is believed to represent the plantation overseer.

Cowhead

His costume is a piece of cloth, which is tied very tightly around the head. On his head is a hat made from half a coconut shell, with real cow horns attached. Facial features are again painted on a wire mesh mask, which covers the face. Cowhead interacts with the audience by charging into them, and keeping them well back from the proceedings. This character seems similar to horned characters in the African tradition, who symbolise powerful people in society.

Belly Woman

This character, as imagined, represents a very heavily pregnant woman. She is an exaggerated and very comical character, played by a man, who elicits lots of laughter from the crowd, as she swings her 'belly' in time with the music.

House or Jawbone Jonkunnu

This character originally wore a terrifying mask, topped by a large and very elaborate plantation house, complete with puppets. He is also known as 'Jawbone', as he originally carried the dried lower jawbone of a horse, along which a piece of wood was scraped to produce a rattling sound. Known as 'Houseboat' today, the mask is not so grotesque.

Set Girls

These characters appear in
pairs, dressed respectively in
blue and red costumes. They too
wear large skirts, with puff-
sleeved tops, lots of jewellery,
large hats and parasols. They
represent the finery of the
European slave-owners. The
word 'set' is believed to have
originated from a term used in
the Quadrille or Square dancing
of colonial times.

Wild Indian

This character possibly originated as a
tribute to the original inhabitants of the
Caribbean islands. He has a headdress made
of feathers which stand erect, mirrors and
pieces of glass, under which he wears black
braided hair. His outfit is made up of
remnants: of food advertisements from
newspapers, Christmas ornaments, and
playing cards.

Koo-Koo or Actor Boy

His outfit is very extravagant and flamboyant, made of silk and satin with lace frills and other forms of finery. He wears a loose jacket over a large skirt. His headdress is made up of mirrors, jewels, and feathers, and is worn over a wig of long curls. Traditionally, he walks very majestically and recites garbled passages from Shakespeare and other famous theatrical pieces.

Sailor

This character wears a white shirt with gold-trimmed sleeves, white trousers, a black tie, and a hat with a gold trim.

Policeman

This character is dressed in a uniform which consists of a black hat with a red band, a red scarf covering his head and neck, a black and white shirt, and black trousers with red stripes down the side of the leg.

Jack-in-the-Green

This character is completely covered with coconut palm leaves. Many Jonkunnu groups have characters who represent the professions in society, and who wear corresponding masks. It is believed that this character belongs to the gardener group. Because of the leaves, he is easily camouflaged and is considered to be a guard for the Set Girls.

Chrismus a come [4]

Chrismus a come, me wan me la-ma,   Chrismus a come, me wan me la-ma,

Chrismus a come, me wan me deggeday,   Chrismus a come, me wan me deggeday.

Chrismus a come, me wan me lama,
Chrismus a come, me wan me lama,
Chrismus a come, me wan me deggeday,
Chrismus a come, me wan me deggeday.

Pretty, pretty gal, me wan me lama,
Pretty, pretty gal, me wan me lama,
Pretty, pretty gal, me wan me deggeday,
Pretty, pretty gal, me wan me deggeday.

Not a shoe to me foot, me wan me lama,
Not a shoe to me foot, me wan me lama,
Pretty, pretty gal, me wan me deggeday,
Pretty, pretty gal, me wan me deggeday.
Not a hat to me head...
Not a bangle to me han...

Activities

- *Create masks and costumes for some of the principal characters of Jonkunnu, and hold your own procession around the school. Ask for donations and raise money for a chosen charity.*

- *Make your own musical instruments using 'found materials' and form a band to accompany the procession. (Make use of your local Scrapstore or Resource Centre for recycled materials.)*

Masks

Masks can be made from a wide variety of materials, and you can create either a very simple or an elaborate design quite easily.

Try using strong, plain paper bags (large enough to cover your head). Cut holes for the eyes and mouth, and decorate by painting, or by sticking on wool or curled paper hair, etc. For eye masks, draw a half design on a piece of card folded in half (to ensure it is symmetrical), then cut it out. Add feathers, sequins, or paint with bright or fluorescent paints, etc. and punch holes at the sides to attach wool, string or ribbon so that your mask can be worn. For whole face masks, cut out a large oval/face shape. Add some depth by either folding the card down the centre, or

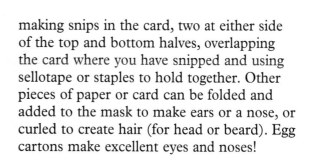

making snips in the card, two at either side of the top and bottom halves, overlapping the card where you have snipped and using sellotape or staples to hold together. Other pieces of paper or card can be folded and added to the mask to make ears or a nose, or curled to create hair (for head or beard). Egg cartons make excellent eyes and noses!

Papier maché

Use wallpaper paste to stick several layers of strips of newspaper over an inflated balloon. Allow to dry. Cut and decorate. Instead of a balloon, try using plasticine or clay moulds. Keep your design as simple as possible, with bold features. Use a generous amount of vaseline, to coat the mould before adding the layers of newspaper, so that it is easy to remove the mask from the mould once it is dry. Be sure to place smaller strips of paper over features such as the eyes and mouth, keeping to the curves to retain them. This type of mask may take a little longer to dry, but the mould can be re-used again and again!

Plaster of Paris

This can be great fun, and the masks created can be very effective and realistic. Use small strips of 'Mod-Roc' (a type of bandage-like material coated with plaster) dipped into water, or small strips of material or bandages dipped in ordinary Plaster of Paris. You can use a mould, a wire mesh frame, a flat surface, or even your face to create your mask. Taking care to protect your face, hair, and clothes, and covering your face with vaseline before starting, get a friend to apply the plaster and cover your whole face, avoiding your eyes and your nostrils (so that you can breathe!). Add a few layers and wait about 15 minutes for the mask to harden. Get the friend to carefully remove it from your face. Allow it to harden some more and use sandpaper to make sure all the edges are smooth. Your mask is now ready to decorate. (This mask can be used as a mould too, when smeared with vaseline, to create other plaster or papier maché masks which will be replicas of the original!)

Musical Instruments

A range of percussion instruments will be a tremendous addition to your procession, as they can be carried and played easily while marching/dancing along. Although there will be no tune, the rhythms can be fantastic!

Shakers

These can be made simply from any kind of container such as plastic bottles, tins, yoghurt pots, with dried beans, peas, rice or pasta inside. Very effective maracas can be made using small balloons and papier maché.(Use PVA rather than wallpaper paste to make them stronger.) A piece of dowelling or similar piece of wood makes a great handle.

Bells

Very carefully (with supervision) use a hammer and nail to make holes in bottle tops and thread these onto strong wire, such as coat-hanger wire. Or a few pierced bottle tops can be nailed to a wooden stick. Add more and decorate the stick. Rhythm sticks can be made by using using two pieces of dowelling, broomstick or curtain pole to knock together. If you use different lengths you will create different sounds.

Scrapers

Find objects with natural ridges or grooves, or make your own by using a saw (again with supervision) to cut chunks out of a piece of wood or bamboo. Use a separate piece of wood to scrape across the grooves to make the sound.

Shaker, bell and scraper

Kwanzaa

Kwanzaa is an African-American festival, based on a combination of East African harvest rituals and the radicalism of the 1960s. The festival was created in 1966 by Dr. Maulana Karenga. Kwanzaa is a means by which Black people are able to celebrate aspects of their heritage and the values of family life, and a time for all Black people to unite and commit themselves to the struggle for equality in an unjust world. It is now celebrated in North America, the Caribbean and many other parts of the African diaspora. By 1988, the *New York Times* reported that as many as 18 million people were observing the festival.

The name kwanzaa comes from the Kiswahili term *matunda ya kwanza*, which translates as 'first fruits of the harvest'. Kiswahili is a trading language with elements of local African languages, Arabic, English and Portuguese that evolved on the East African coast, and is widely spoken today in Kenya, Tanzania and northern Mozambique. Kwanzaa is a festival that runs over seven days, from 26 December to 1 January, with each day focusing on a particular 'Principle'. Collectively the seven Principles are called *Nguzo Saba*, and give guidance for how life should be lived.

In addition to the seven Principles are seven Symbols, which are derived from East African culture and which have significant meanings.

During Kwanzaa, followers greet each other with the Swahili greeting *Habari gani?* which means 'What's happening?' or 'What's the news?', to which the reply given is a different one of the Principles for each of the days of Kwanzaa (see opposite).

The home is decorated with the symbols of Kwanzaa, and other decorations with an African motif. The colours of Kwanzaa are black, red and green, and homes are decorated with balloons, streamers, flowers and such like, in these colours.

Kwanzaa Karamu

The festival ends with a feast (Karamu), which is held on 31 December. Whether held in the home or a community venue, this event is a co-operative effort, with an on-going programme of entertainment and ceremony.

A large *mkeka* (see below) is placed on the floor, where all the food is attractively arranged, and from which people help themselves. The programme follows a traditional pattern consisting of: welcoming, remembering, reassessment and recommitment, rejoicing, a farewell statement and a call to unity to conclude.

Seven Principles (Nguzo Saba)

Umoja (OO-MA-JAH) – Unity
Reflected in the African saying 'I am we' or 'I am because We are', this principle stresses the importance of the family, community, nation and race coming together. The legendary African American boxer Muhammad Ali once put his own spin on this saying: when asked to give a poem in a press conference, he said 'Me – We'; this was later described by the American novelist Normal Mailer as perhaps the most concise poem ever composed in the English language.

Kujichagulia (KOO-GEE-CHA-GOO-LEE-YAH) – Self-determination
This principle encourages people of African descent to define themselves and their needs, and work towards making decisions in their own best interest.

Ujima (OO-GEE-MAH) – Collective work and responsibility
This principle encourages people in the community and wider afield to work together to solve the problems they face.

Ujamaa (OO-JAH-MAH) – Co-operative economics
This principle recognises the collective economic strength of the community, and encourages mutual support for business and the ability for everyone to benefit from the profits.

Nia (NEE-YAH) – Purpose
This principle encourages individuals to be self-reflective and to set themselves personal goals, which will also benefit the community.

Kuumba (KOO-OOM-BAH) – Creativity
This principle encourages individuals to do all that they can to build and maintain the community.

Imani (EE-MAH-NEE) – Faith
This principle focuses on the community members believing in themselves and their ability to succeed and be victorious in their righteous struggle.

The seven symbols of Kwanzaa

Mkeka (M-kay-cah)

The *mkeka* is a placemat (preferably of straw) on which all the other symbols are placed. It is a symbol of tradition and therefore demonstrates that tradition should be the foundation for everything else.

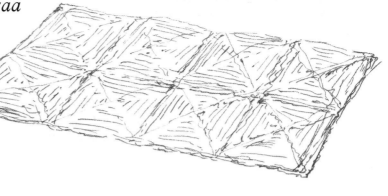

Mazao (Mah-zay-oh)

Fruits, vegetable and nuts, which represent crops.

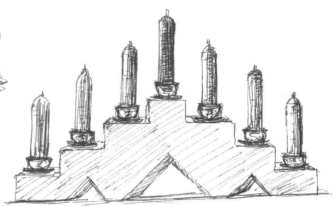

Kinara (Kee-nah-rah)

The *kinara* is a candle-holder for seven candles and it represents the stalk from which everyone sprang.

Mshumaa Saba (Mee-shoo-maah)

The seven candles represent the Seven Principles. One is lit each day beginning with the black candle in the centre, which is lit on Unity Day. Then the first red candle is lit (all red candles are on the left of the centre candle), and then a first green candle on the third day (all green candles are on the right), then red, green, red, green. On the day of Imani, all seven candles will be burning.

Vibunzi/Muhindi (Moo-heen-dee)

The ear of corn represents the offspring (children) of the stalk (father). The significance is that the ear of corn itself has the ability to become a stalk, and produce more offspring, etc., ensuring the continuation of the nation. One ear of corn is placed on the mat for each child of the house, and at least one, even if there are none, to acknowledge unrealised potential and the African concept of social parenthood.

Kikombe Cha Umoja (Kee-coam-bay chah-oo-moe-jah)

The communal Unity Cup symbolises the first Principle of Kwanzaa. It is used to pour the libation (drink offering) for the ancestors. Each family member drinks from it to honour ancestors and commit themselves to the struggle begun by their ancestors.

Zawadi (Sah-wah-dee)

These are presents or gifts, exchanged between parents and children, usually home-made. Children often receive a book to symbolise the African value and tradition of learning, and some kind of heritage symbol. They are usually exchanged on the last day of Kwanzaa, 1 January, but can be given at any time.

Other symbols include:

Bendera Ya Taifa

The flag of Black Nationalism which symbolises the struggle for freedom and equality, based on the colours that Marcus Garvey determined as national colours for African people throughout the world.

> Black – Black people
> Red – The blood of the ancestors
> Green – Land, life and new ideas

Harambee

Swahili for 'Let's pull together'. A toast, said each day seven times, as everyone drinks in turn from the *kikombe*.

Kwanzaa Karamu Programme
(from a model by Dr. Karenga)

Kukaribisha *(Welcoming)*
Introduction. Welcome of distinguished guests and all Elders.
Cultural expression: songs, music, group dancing, poetry, performances.

Kukumbuka *(Remembering)*
Reflections of a Man, Woman and Child.
Cultural expression.

Kuchunguza Tena Na Kutoa Ahadi Tena *(Reassessment and Recommitment)*
Introduction of a guest speaker or family elder and a short talk.

Kushangilla *(Rejoicing)*

Tamshi la Tambiko *(Libation Statement)*
The communal cup is filled with juice or water (water is suggested as it holds the essence of life) and is poured in the direction of the four winds; north, south, east and west, before being passed to family members or guests, who either sip or make the gesture of sipping.

LIBATION STATEMENT
For the Motherland cradle of civilisation.
For the ancestors and their indomitable spirit.
For the elders from whom we can learn much.
For our youth who represent the promise for tomorrow.
For our people the original people.
For our struggle and in remembrance of those who have struggled on our behalf.
For Umoja the principle of unity which should guide us in all that we do.
For the creator who provides all things great and small.

Kikombe Cha Umoja *(The passing round of the Unity Cup)*

Kutoa Majina *(List of names of family ancestors and black heroes)*

Ngoma *(Drum song)*

Karamu *(Dinner feast)*

Tamshi la Tutaonana *(Farewell statements from the elders)*

The Day of Meditation (Siku ya Taamuli)

New Year's Day, 1 January, is the last day of Kwanzaa. As with other people around the world who make New Year resolutions, African people are asked to reflect on the past and on the future, focusing not just on themselves, but also their communities. However, this quiet reflection can be traced back to being an integral part of the first-fruits harvest celebrations of the Akan people. Three Kawaida questions are asked:

Who am I?
Am I really who I say I am?
Am I all I ought to be?

Although growing in popularity, Kwanzaa is not without its critics. Some African-Americans view the festival as paganistic, being particularly critical of the libation ceremony in which ancestors are worshipped and seen as intercessors between followers and God. Others see it as anti-Christian, an alternative to Christmas introduced to diminish the true meaning of Christmas, especially as it begins on 26 December. Its origin in East Africa is also seen by some as making it less relevant, as most African-Americans have their ethnic origins in West Africa.

Activity

- *Weave a mkeka (see below), using paper or strips of cloth in the symbolic colours of black, red, and green.*

How to make a mkeka

You will need:
Sugar paper in green, yellow, red and black (whatever size you want)
Pencil/ruler/scissors

Fold the black sugar paper in half.
Draw lines at 2.5cm intervals from the fold to within 2cm of the outside edge.

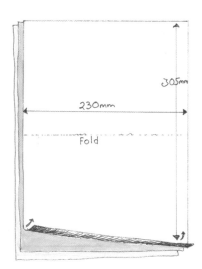

Cut along these lines from the fold to the 2cm gap from the edge.

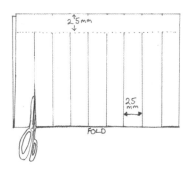

Cut the green, yellow and red papers into 2cm strips.
Weave the coloured strips in and out of the black strips alternating the colours to give the mat a pattern.

Glue the coloured strips at the end to secure to the black sheet of paper. Alternatively, use different coloured ribbons to add additional interest.

> ## *Activities*
>
> - *Design a programme for a Karamu feast.*
>
> - *Make and play an Oware game (see below).*

Oware

The mathematical game of Oware or Ayo as it is sometimes known, which may well be one of the oldest games in the world, is played not just in West Africa, but all over Africa and is known as *Mankala* in East Africa and *Ohoro* in South Africa. Other names for the game are *Awale, Awelo, Ourin* and *Wari* (Caribbean). It has many variations, relating mainly to the number of rows (5/6/7) on the board and to how the game ends. In traditional settings it can be found played in hollowed-out scoops of earth with pebbles, in rings of sand with cowrie or other shells, or on specially carved wooden boards with seeds.

Items needed to play

48 small smooth stones, beans, beads or cowrie shells. You could even use marbles – but this is less traditional!
14-cup Oware board – or use egg cartons or any found object that could be adapted in this way

How to make an Oware board

You will need:
48 small stones, beans, beads or shells
2 egg boxes (one dozen and one six-egg size)
Glue/stapler/acrylic paint

Cut the lid of the large egg box and glue it to the underside of the egg portion of the box.
Cut out two extra egg sections from the smaller box and staple one at the centre of each end of the larger box.
Paint the gameboard. Why not choose the black, red and green?

Oware board

How to play

Two players (Player A and Player B)
Objective: to be the player with the most
stones in your bank at the end of the
game.

1. Place four beans in the bottom of each of
   the 14 cups.
2. Play:

Player A picks up all the stones from any cup
on his/her side of the board. Starting with
the next cup to the right (anti-clockwise),
Player A drops one stone at a time into each
successive cup. After dropping the last stone
in a cup, Player A picks up all the stones in
THAT cup and continues to drop one in
each consecutive cup. Player A's turn ends
when he/she puts the last seed in an empty
cup. (Player A has the longest first turn.)

Player B then chooses any cup of stones and
begins a turn exactly like Player A's. A player
scores when he/she drops the last stone in a
cup with THREE others (making FOUR
stones in a cup). The player then puts all
four stones in his/her bank'. (See
illustration.)

If the player puts a stone in a cup with three
others and it is not the last stone, the other
player puts the four stones in his/her bank.

The game ends when a player finds no
stones left to move on his/her side. The other
player gets the remaining stones on the
board. The player who has accumulated the
most stones in his/her bank, WINS!

Section Three

Music, Dance and the Oral Tradition

Music, dance and poetry or storytelling are almost always connected in African society. Handed down from generation to generation, these traditional art forms are central to daily life, so much so that many African languages do not even have a specific noun for 'music'.

From a very early age, the African child in a traditional community was introduced to community life by listening to the sounds and rhythms of many different drums beating out at religious and social events in the village, taking part in dances, making and playing musical instruments, and playing musical games. Through his participation in these events he would learn about the history of his people, the rules that enabled him to be a good citizen, farming methods and how to measure the time by the seasons or by the moon. He would also develop a wonderful sense of melody and rhythm. We use the past tense because, although there remain many African societies where this is still the predominant mode of education, cultural change and globalisation are altering this means of understanding the world and our place in it.

African music is a mix of natural sounds, including the spoken word, and music. Though its instruments are similar to those used in Western music – namely wind, string and percussion – they are combined in a way that is totally different. In traditional African music each sound has a specific, life-related meaning. Some westerners complain of the lack of 'control' in the music, though this reflects their own culture more than the music itself.

The role of the drum in African music is literally sacred – this is particularly the case with the *djembe* (jem-bay), which originated in West African countries such as Guinea, Senegal and Mali. The drum acts as a tool for communication in society; it may call forth various spirits and beings; its most important significance lies in the celebration of a variety of religious and secular events such as naming ceremonies, rites of passage, gatherings for engagements and weddings, seasonal rejoicing such as harvest or after a drought, and in warrior rituals.

The role of the professional musician, or *griot*, is to communicate history and tradition. These musicians travel the countryside and recount the histories of their people, again with music at the very heart of their craft. In traditional African societies the *griots* were treated with fear and often contempt. They lived in settlements separate from the rest of the population, and could not walk on the streets in the presence of the king; their bodies were not buried in the community cemetery plots, but were left in the hollowed out trunks of giant grey baobab trees. Indeed, their position was such that the first Portuguese arriving in West Africa in the 15th century, seeing them inhabiting their own 'ghettos', called them 'Jews'.

Religiosity also has music and dance at its heart. The masked and costumed dancers of the masquerade 'become' the spirits of African traditional religion in both their public ceremonies and rituals, and in their private secret societies, to ensure continued good relations with ancestors. They bring the necessary spirits to life through their sounds and movements, working themselves into a possessed state.

It was inevitable that the majority of slaves originating from the 3000 mile coastline between Northern Senegal and Southern Angola, who were transported to the Caribbean and the Americas, would take their music, dance and traditional storytelling skills with them. It was also inevitable that these surviving traditions would be subject to varying degrees of change and adaptation in their new environments.

In this chapter we trace the origin of these traditions in Africa, and, as with the previous section, follow its evolution in both the past and the present, from Africa to the Caribbean and beyond.

The oral tradition – griots

When an old man dies, a library burns

Malian writer, Amadon Hampate Ba

In modern times, the printed page, television, films and radio have all but replaced the storyteller, but storytelling is the oldest of art forms. The aboriginal peoples of Australia believed that the storyteller could literally sing the world into existence, recreating it with his 'songline'. Peoples reinvented their histories and their identities through the shared memory preserved by the storytellers. They preserved valuable information and folk memory that would otherwise have been lost.

Likewise, the telling of stories, proverbs and riddles was one of the main ways in which African communities passed on their culture and history. Nothing was written, and so even today the oral story in Africa has the same sort of authority as western societies accord to written documents. All that was necessary for moral, social and spiritual guidance was passed down by word of mouth from one generation to another in stories, dances, songs and ceremonies, and through the teachings of priests, the head of the family, chiefs and professional genealogists and musicians called *griots* (or *jalis*).

The absence of written records is easily explained. The presence of Arabic in the Sahara region meant that writing was associated with the Koran and so was seen as sacred; those who could write were seen as having ritual powers, not as transmitting information. Meanwhile, the only other script in the region was Amharic, the alphabet used in Ethiopia and Eritrea. These ancient Christian cultures did keep written records, but saw themselves – and were seen – as very different to much of the rest of sub-Saharan Africa.

There is a famous modern illustration of the nature of griots and storytelling. Alex Haley, who wrote the bestselling narrative *Roots: The Saga of an American Family* (later dramatised for television), had a remarkable encounter with an old *griot* in 1966. Haley was an African-American attempting to research the ancestry of his ancestors who had been shipped as slaves across the Atlantic. While researching his maternal ancestry, his search had taken him to the small village of Juffure in The Gambia. There he found a *griot* who gave an oral account of seven previous generations of Mandinka tribal history, including the disappearance of 16 year-old Kunta Kinte, who had disappeared in the forest whilst searching for wood to make a drum. Kunta Kinte was his enslaved ancestor. His fact-finding mission had provided the missing link that verified the stories told to him during his childhood by his grandmother.

The old griot had talked for nearly two hours up to then, '…the oldest of these four sons, Kunta, went away from his village and was never seen again'… I sat as if I were carved of stone. My blood seemed to have congealed. This man whose lifetime had been in this back-country African village had no way in the world to know that he had just echoed what I had heard all through my boyhood years on my grandma's front porch in Henning, Tennessee.

Kunta Kinte's desire to make the drum – the most basic form of musical connection with the ancestors – had forged an entirely different type of tradition; one that blended the suffering of slaves with the inevitable legend of the drum.

Griots are really, then, jacks of all trades. They are historians, genealogists, musicians and poets. They can recall the history of their people for centuries, and the lineage of the kings and royalty of their nations, and thus can tell stories which last several days. They can trace their heritage back to the 12th century and the rule of the legendary emperor of the ancient kingdom of Mali, Sundiata, the (original) Lion King. Even today, in countries such as Senegal and Mali, *griots* can be found who can sing of the magical battle between Sundiata and his rival Sumanguru – both men used spells as they sought the upper hand. As *griots* sing, there is no doubt that they feel they are reawakening those ancient events to life.

It was natural that, in a culture with no written language until Muslim traders brought Arabic writing to the area, those who had good memories came to hold a very important position in society. They were the living archives who recorded customs, traditions, and the governmental principles of kings. They travelled from village to village, singing the news, the history of the tribe, traditional folktales and accompanying themselves on the *kora*, the *djembe* and *sabar* (drums), and the *balafon*. Their tales and their music were the fibres that bound the nation together; indeed, we can speculate that this very importance to society was what led to ostracising of the *griot* caste. They were so powerful that they were to be feared, and set aside.

Yet, like all historians, what they tended to record were 'official' histories, rather than truths. In southern Senegal today, *griots* sing of the great and noble deeds of one Abdou Ndiaye, who, it is said, journeyed into the neighbouring country of Guinea-Bissau, brought people onto his side and won victories in the holy name of Islam. Yet according to written records, Abdou Ndiaye was in fact a collaborator with the Portuguese colonialists in the early 20th century, whose collusion indirectly led to the deaths of many who resisted colonial power.

In Sundiata's time, *griots* taught princes and advised kings. Later, wealthy families would employ them to advise and help them in their negotiations with other families. They would also engage in praise-singing; composing and performing songs of praise for royal or wealthy patrons. In return for what they had to offer, they gained money and a great deal of respect. Rewards were also often given in the form of the social custom of 'dashing' or 'spraying'. Guests at social functions would show off their wealth, generosity and social status by showering money on performers. The money would be stuck on sweaty foreheads, tucked into the instruments or simply showered over their heads as they played. But *griots* were also feared. Upsetting a *griot* might encourage him to compose a song which mocked or cursed the subject, bringing bad luck.

By virtue of their role and social position, the *griot* caste is a tradition passed from one generation to another, generally from father to son. Even today the famous *griots* of West Africa – the Kouyates and Diabates – belong to the same lineages of ancient musicians and praise-singers. Training begins within the family, from *griot* parents, followed by attendance at a formal *griot* school and an apprenticeship to a master *griot*. There are

also *griottes* (female *griots*) whose importance is recognised in the existence of female epics. These encourage independence and self-reliance; giving comfort and empowerment to other women, especially in the area of relationships. *Griottes* traditionally sing at ceremonies and special celebrations. For example, when a woman is to be married, they will sing to her to prepare her for her new life and the troubles that may lie ahead. *Griottes* have a more important role today than in the past, when due to family obligations they had less freedom to travel, often standing by as a *griot* recited and singing only short choruses. Today some of the most famous praise-singers of West Africa are *griottes*: Kandia Kouyate and Oumou Sangare are just two names that spring to mind.

The ancient art of the *griot*, *jeliya*, is still practised today and *griots* remain the preservers of Mandinka oral history and musical tradition (see below). This was once illustrated in the unlikely setting of Barbican Hall, London. In the late 1990s, when Kandia Kouyate gave a concert there, the security guards were presented with an unexpected problem. As the overwhelming voice of Kouyate filled the hall, various West African members of the audience rose and made their way to the front of the theatre; dancing onto the stage, they had come to deposit money into the folds of Kouyate's yellow dress. At first, a guard tried to intervene, but the situation was too unusual for him; ancient cultural norms proved impossible to overturn, even in the heart of secular, late 20th century London.

Though the old traditions remain, the passing of time and development in travel and communication have transformed the *griot* and his craft. European colonisation, and the move from a traditional rural existence to a modern urban environment, have caused the *griot* to adapt. West African culture has absorbed other influences in terms of music and instruments. Modern technology has developed and given the *griot* a global audience. Today *griots* still write praise-songs and sing commercials for businesses, government agencies and political candidates. Some contemporary artists, such as the Senegalese singer Youssou N'Dour, may not describe themselves as *griots*, but they still perform similar roles in society, providing music for social and political events, rites of passage and for the purpose of praise. Youssou N'Dour's grandmother came from a *griot* family, and it is believed that she taught him all of his songs.

Top *griot* recordings include:

> Toumani Diabate – Nouvelles Cordes
>   Anciennes, Djelika, Kaira
> Kandia Kouyate – Kita Kan
> Tata Dindin – The Gambia

Musical instruments
The djembe (or jembe)

The *djembe* is a goblet-shaped wooden drum, now stringed with goat-skin, although originally with antelope skin. Its base is made from the hollowed-out trunk of Lenke wood (a hard wood found only in Sub-Saharan Africa). The skin is stretched across the head and traditionally tightened with a cord of twisted fur, although modern plastic cords are now used. It is both a solo and accompanying instrument. A traditional drum ensemble consists of two *djembes* and three bass drums: the *dununba*, a low, deep drum, the *sangban* and the *kenkeni*. The *djembe* is played with the hands, and usually at an angle to allow the sound to be fully released from the base of the drum. It is usually held between the knees, although soloists often play it standing, when it hangs from the upper part of the body, fixed with belts. Three distinct sounds or tones can be achieved by hitting the drum in different places and in different ways. A bass tone comes from the centre of the drum, and two other tones from the side of the drum, when played with fingers either closed or splayed. These three sounds, multiplied by the number of drums being played, are utilised in an infinite variety of ways to create fascinating rhythms, which can last for as long as 20 minutes and be played at varying speeds.

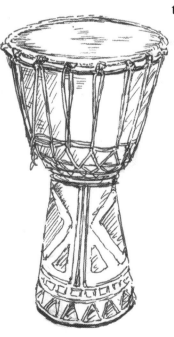

The kora

The *kora* is a 'harp lute'. It has a wide range of sounds and notes. Each *kora* is different and is made especially for the person who plays it. Traditionally it has 21 strings: 11 played by the left hand and 10 by the right. It is tuned like a guitar, by tightening and loosening the strings, and is played using both thumbs and both forefingers simultaneously. Its sound is very much like that of the harp, but the intricate way in which it is played is more like the flamenco guitar. The body of the *kora* is made from a large *calabash* cut in half and partially covered with calf skin.

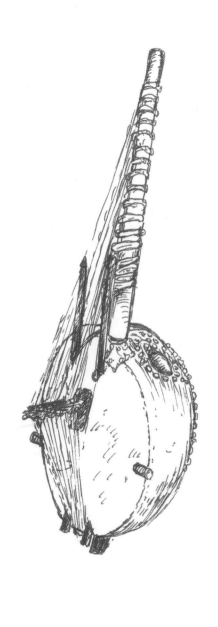

Kora player

The balafon

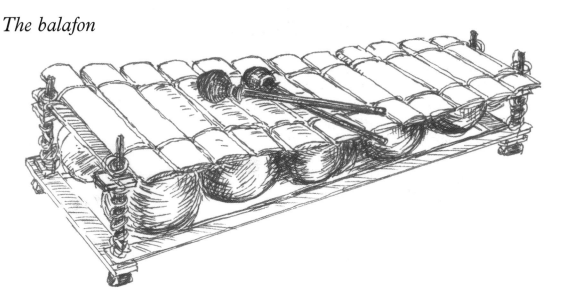

The *balafon* is a particular type of *marimba*, or xylophone. *Marimbas* are found throughout the continent of Africa and vary in shape, size and sound. Each consist of a set of 18-21 tone bars or keys, cut from slowly seasoned rose or bene wood, arranged from low to high notes, and laid across a bamboo frame. Different sized gourds act as amplifiers, altering the volume and pitch of each note. They are played by striking them with a mallet. The gourds used in the *balafon* have holes in them.

In West Africa, Guinea in particular, the *balafon* belongs to the tradition of the Mandinka people, and the *griot*. The story of the *Sosso balafon*, an integral part of the story of Sundiata, helps us to understand the links between this ancient instrument and the modern nation of Guinea.

The story of Sundiata

Much of what we know about Sundiata comes from the stories handed down by *griots* from generation to generation.

The legend of Sundiata, The Lion King, is a powerful tale of courage and determination. Born the son of a Mandinka warrior, he is driven into exile with his mother by a rival queen. Overcoming both physical and political obstacles, he goes on to claim his rightful throne, becoming the liberator and founder of the great empire of Mali ('where the king resides'). The story is full of supernatural happenings as Sundiata and his *griot*, Balla Fassete, embark upon a series of adventures. Readers and listeners are left with the message that greatness involves working with others and remaining hopeful in the face of adversity.

Activities

- Read the story of the original Lion King, Sundiata.

- Read the words of the traditional folk song, 'Wake Nicodemus' by the anti-slavery advocate, Henry Clay Work (see below). What evidence is there to suggest that Nicodemus may have been a griot?

Wake Nicodemus

Nicodemus the slave was of African birth,
And was bought for a bagful of gold;
He was reckoned as part of the salt of the earth,
But he died years ago, very old.
'Twas his last sad request – so we laid him away
In the trunk of an old hollow tree.
Wake me up! was his charge, at the first break of day;
Wake me up for the Great Jubilee!

Chorus:
The Good Time Coming is almost here!
It was long – long – long on the way!
Now, go tell Elijah to hurry up, Pomp,
And meet us at the gum tree down in the swamp
To wake Nicodemus today.

He was known as a prophet – at least was as wise –
For he told of the battles to come;
And we trembled with dread when he roll'd up his eyes,
And we heeded the shake of his thumb.
Though he clothed us with fear, yet the garments he wore
Were in patches at elbow and knee;
And he still wears the suit that he wore long ago
As he sleeps in the old hollow tree.

Nicodemus was never the sport of the lash,
Though the bullet has oft cross'd his path;
There were none of his masters so brave or so rash
As to face such a man in his wrath.
Yet his great heart with kindness was filled to the brim –
He obeyed who was born to command;
But he long'd for the morning which then was so dim,
For the morning which now is at hand.

'Twas a long, weary night – we were almost in fear
That the future was more than he knew;
'Twas a long, weary night, but the morning is near,
And the words of our prophet are true.
There are signs in the sky that the darkness is gone;
There are wonders in endless array!
While the storm (which had seemingly banished the dawn)
Only hastens the advent of day.

Henry Clay Work, 1864

Masquerade

Impersonation and mimicry thrive in many cultures, but the form that such customs take in Africa is unique, and is summed up in the word 'masquerade'. We encountered examples of this in the last section, for instance in the Jonkunnu festival (see p.60) Here people do not impersonate one another but rather assume the form of powerful presences from the spirit world, and so act as a bridge between the worlds of the living and the dead. In African society, where ancestors and family members are always present in the collective mind, whether living or dead, the masquerade therefore has a crucial function: it is a constant reminder of the presence of invisible beings and realities – though the masquerade itself is passionately, gloriously, visible.

There are many varieties of masquerade, but the idea that binds them together is that someone adopts the form of a particular sacred spirit or deity by putting on the 'mask' of the spirit. They adopt the spirit's powers, and can transform themselves, and others, through the new powers that the mask confers. Masks are therefore incredibly powerful symbols in Africa, and not to be worn lightly. Masquerades are complex and very diverse in practice, but all play a central role in society. As many mask-making African societies did not have a written language, the masquerade was one of the ways of passing on their cultural and religious heritage.

Though the mask is the best-known aspect of the masquerade, the costumes used involve many other elements. The person adopting the masquerade will be covered in special clothes, beads and ornaments, each of which has a point of contact with a sacred element of the spirit behind the masquerade. The spectacle of the masquerade is, therefore, a unique experience.

Modern life has of course diluted aspects of the masquerade tradition. In some places it is used as a form of tourist attraction, and in others masks are made smoother and flatter so as to be more readily displayed on walls, and so more easily commercialised. Still, ancient masquerade traditions continue to thrive in many parts of Africa, especially where these are connected to initiation and funerary rites.

Masquerades are performed for many reasons. Often they are associated with marking the transitions in the life cycle. As boys and girls reach adulthood, this period of their life and the changes it brings are celebrated and they are taught the skills to become adults. At funeral ceremonies, the masquerade assists the passing of the dead into the afterlife. There are masquerades that show respect for those spirits who bring wealth and prosperity to the community. Others honour women and the powerful role they play in society as childbearers, and there are ceremonies to aid fertility. Harvest time is another occasion for honouring the spirits, and ensuring plenty of crops and animals. Masquerades are also a time when the community asks for the help and protection of spirits in everyday living: from illness, wars and disasters. Spirits are invoked to settle legal disputes and parcel out blame in criminal matters. However, some masquerades are simply celebrations: of ancestors, weddings, festivals, royal occasions and religious events.

The masquerader in traditional African societies is usually male, although the mask he wears can be either male or female. Women, although they sometimes are involved in making the costumes, in providing their clothes for the female masks, or in singing and dancing alongside the masqueraders, often simply make up the audience. If they are allowed to see the performance at all, they have to keep their distance, as they are thought to be in danger from the masquerade. One exception to this rule is found among the Sande Secret Society of the Mende people of Sierra Leone. During the initiation ceremony of this all-female society, which teaches young girls the skills and knowledge of womanhood, the spirit Sowei manifests itself to young women to aid their transition. The mask worn (by a woman) during the ceremony represents the perfect woman: it has a very elaborate hairstyle, delicate facial features and a row of rings on the neck.

Masquerades fall into two main categories: some are associated with social rituals, and others with personal rituals. In the former, they manifest themselves at public events where the masked dancers perform in front of an audience which joins in. In the latter, they are private events and the dancers belong to a religious society, which keeps its knowledge secret. These 'secret' societies exist for many purposes, ranging from keeping dead ancestors happy to bringing success in war and in hunting, and providing protection against illness or bad luck. They are most common today in the area of Sierra Leone.

The making of masks is an art. They are made by specialists in this field, or by skilled craftsmen such as carvers or blacksmiths. Blacksmiths in particular occupy a significant role in society, in part through their importance in connection with masquerades. In Mende societies, blacksmiths are seen as having a special channel of communication to the unseen world, and are treated with both reverence and suspicion. As with the *griots*, they form a 'caste' by virtue of their occupation, or social role. However, although the tradition of mask-making is usually passed from father to son, in some parts of Africa it is possible to become an apprentice. Apprenticeships can last for as long as three years, and apprentices pay for the privilege of their training.

The particular types of masks created have changed little over time, usually falling into three categories: face masks that are worn vertically on the face; those worn like a helmet over the whole head; and head-dresses, worn high on top of the head, with a transparent material attached and covering the face, such as a mesh type of veil, raffia or grass. Some masks take the form of humans, often with very stylised features which represent the concepts of beauty or strength. Others take the form of, or combinations of, animals considered to be powerful, such as the elephant, the antelope or the hawk, or possess both animal and human features, together with the resulting combination of powers. Masks vary in size as well as shape. Some are very small, just covering the face of the wearer, while others are enormous. One particular mask worn by the Bwa people, of Burkina Faso and Mali, is over six feet tall, and thus requires the wearer to be someone with great strength.

Mask makers are often believed to have been strongly influenced by the spirit powers of the image they create. For example, some peoples in Mali believe that mask-makers have the capacity to use the powers of the mask to harm someone. This follows from the belief that there are spirit powers present in everything, and therefore that masks are created in the knowledge that they will house the spirit power of whatever material they are made from. This inevitably means that, like blacksmiths, mask-makers are treated with both awe and wariness, and need to tread carefully between the demands of the seen and unseen worlds.

A huge range of materials is used to make and embellish the mask. Those made from wood are carved from a single piece, with a tool called an *adze*, and the finer details are added with a knife. But masks are also made from metal, fur, shells, beads, bells, raffia and feathers. A mask will often be made in private and an elder will be called upon to carry out a ceremony to enable it to be empowered by a spirit. Similarly, when a mask is no longer needed, the elder will perform another ceremony to withdraw the power of the particular spirit.

Animal mask

Hand mask

Mendi mask

As these spirit powers are considered to be quite unpredictable, elaborate rituals, taboos and restrictions have grown up around the making and handling of masks, to protect their makers and wearers, and to ensure that the spirits they house are as powerful as they can be. Through the mask, pleas can then be made to these powers to bring good fortune in all areas of life.

When all the preparations have been completed, there is nothing quite like watching a masquerade performance. The masquerader dances everywhere: in and around sacred places, in the streets and the areas in which people live. Dressing in private and ensuring that his whole body is covered with the complete costume of the masquerade – constructed of a combination of wood, paint, fibre, shells, hide and cloth – so that no one can recognise him, the wearer loses his own identity and 'becomes', as if in a trance, the spirit that the mask represents, with all of the characteristics of that spirit. He is a kind of 'psychic medium'. Beginning with what he knows about the particular spirit, a ceremony might start with the masquerader acting out well-known stories and known aspects of the spirit's character. He then takes the performance a stage further, improvising, and making a 'leap into the unknown'. His audience has a part to play. The audience recognises the persona of the mask, whether a spirit, ancestor, animal or otherwise, and the purpose of its visitation, and whether that persona is friendly, to be revered or viewed as fearful – and reacts in the appropriate manner.

The performance provides a form of entertainment, although the function it serves is quite serious: reaffirming the social order by enabling communication between the past and the present and between humans and nature. As masks therefore have a complex and multiple function, their mere display in Western museums cannot begin to illustrate their meaning.

Given all the different strands of belief, tradition and memory that are blended into the masquerade, you can imagine the power of the event. The inanimate world comes alive, is literally personified, and the constant struggle and exchange between the worlds of the living and the dead is embodied before the audience's gaze!

(See also 'Carnival', p.116-22.)

Activities [5]

- Visit the African Rooms at the British Museum, London, to find out more about masquerades.

- In groups, think of all the differences between masks in the West and in Africa. What makes African masks special?

Drums

God is dumb, until the drum speaks
Drum is the ear of God

Traditional proverbs

There is no precise word for 'music' in any
African language. Music is not merely
concerned with entertainment, but is central
to the fabric of life. First and foremost it is
participatory. Music, song and rhythm are a
feature of many daily activities, and almost
every special event has music and dance at
its core. Everyone will join in, whether
playing an instrument, singing, dancing,
clapping, or watching and passing opinion on
the proceedings. The role of music is vast in
traditional Africa. Some of the purposes for
which it is used are: to evoke deities, to
empower, to praise, to pass on historical
knowledge and myths, for healing,
celebration, and courtship, to
draw communities together,
to criticise, to teach and to
entertain.

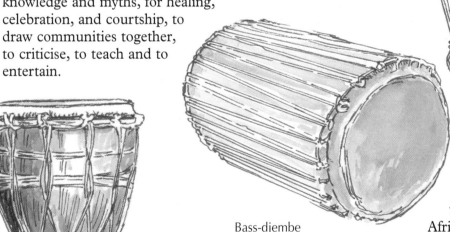

Drum

Bass-djembe

Djembe

At the heart,
though, of what we
think of as 'music' in
African societies is the
drum. Possibly the world's oldest instrument,
nowhere has the drum more significance or
purpose than in African society. It is much
more than a mere instrument. The drum
provides the rhythm or pulse of the music.
Within many festivals, the beat of the drum
was used to communicate the particular
dance which was to be performed for that
particular event or occasion, such as the
birth of a child or to celebrate a marriage.

People attending the event took their cues from the force and rhythm of the drumbeats, the type of rhythm changing with each situation. Most importantly, there was a clear distinction between music for rituals and music for social occasions.

The drum beats with the heart of the world, and is an essential ingredient to much ritual. One of the most powerful descriptions of the use of drums in rituals comes in Malidoma Patrice Somé's *Like Water of the Spirit*. Malidoma – a Dagara from Burkina Faso – recounts how, during the initiation period for adolescent boys, some of the most powerful rituals which he and his fellow Dagara went through started with a combination of drumbeats and other traditional practices.

The drum was traditionally much more than a mere instrument or even something inherent in social situations or rituals. In folklore it is linked with stories of the creation of the world. The drum was also a more direct form of communication, a substitute for speech – the 'talking drum'. These 'talking drums' – *tabas* in Wolof – were used to send and receive messages, in code, over long distances. In widespread use across West Africa, they are typically small drums, designed in an hourglass shape, which can be strapped over the shoulder and played with ease. They produce a staccato, rattling rhythm, as opposed to the deeper bass notes of the *djembes*. Although people have moved on to the telephone from the talking drum, their distinctive rhythms can be heard across West African cities to this day, an illustration of their continued cultural importance.

The shapes and types of drums found in particular regions of Africa, and their use, are highly varied, and so it is very difficult to make generalisations. The nuances of style in drumming can only be found in the minds of master drummers, whose artistry is said to die with them. They are believed to have a spiritual relationship with their drum, and although they train pupils, each master drummer must ultimately forge his own relationship with his art: ultimately it is not something that can be taught, but only felt and intuited. This is why any modern attempts to copy or inappropriately use others' styles are viewed with great contempt. The American musician, Paul Simon, found this when he used African drumming styles and techniques in his work.

Despite the variations across the continent of Africa, there are some common features. Drumming is, almost without exception, a night-time activity. Only during periods of mourning or days of rest is it performed during daylight hours. Occasionally, as dusk nears, you will see groups of men gathering with *djembes* and beginning to beat out a rhythm; but usually the drumbeats are heard only at night, in preparation for a festival or during a celebration.

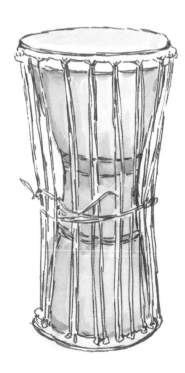

Talking drum

Ben Baddoo: a master drummer speaks

I STARTED *playing the drums when I was six years old. We lived in Nsakina, a village about 20 miles from Accra, the capital of Ghana. As the Chieftain of the village, my grandfather co-ordinated many rituals together with my great-aunt, herself a priestess. All of these rituals were accompanied by drumming and everyone was expected to play the drums. It was just what you did.*

Sometimes, during a particularly powerful ritual, the drumming would carry on without stopping for one or two weeks. During these rituals, my older brothers would initially hand me a bottle, or even a cowbell, to play out the rhythms. If one of them got off their chair to go to the kitchen, then I'd take my chance and go for the drums. Within two years, I was actually a very good drummer.

Because drumming is so important in calling the gods and the spirits of our forefathers to the present earthly sphere, young and beautiful priestesses often marry old master drummers of the clan or village. It is said the gods often possess people with lovely singing voices and this blends well with good drumming in calling forth the spirits.

When someone becomes possessed they leave this world and using drumming as a vehicle travel through the spirit world. My great-aunt was said to ride with our drumming, and she changed her voice according to the part of the spirit world that she found herself in. Sometimes during her journey the drumming would suddenly stop and she would greet the participants in clear English or French to indicate that she was in either England or France, even though she was illiterate and had never been to school, could not read or write and had never learnt these languages.

When I was 10 years old, I left the village to go and live with my mother in Accra. With such an intense childhood experience of drums, they were never far from my thoughts. In my late teens

I joined a troupe that were funded by the Arts Council of Ghana, taking up the drums once more. Before long, the head of the troupe realised that I was actually a fairly gifted drummer and soon I was leading the drummers. I eventually established my own group of drummers, Sankofa, and we toured all over Ghana.

In 1984, we were invited to come to the UK by an English visitor. I was 25 years old and our prospects were great. We performed at the Cambridge Theatre in London's West End. As we were the only African drumming group in the UK at the time, we were a real hit. I joined forces with Peter Blackman, who had good relations with the Arts Council of England, and set up Steel and Skin Limited which toured around the schools and community centres of the UK offering workshops in African drumming and dance.

Over the years I've learned a huge repertoire of rhythms to accompany the many traditional dances that we have in our culture. To be recognised as a master drummer, you need to have worked under the continuous supervision of a master drummer. I did that whilst leading my own dance group there in my early 20s. It's really very hard work as there are so many variations and arrangements to keep in your head. None of this is written down. To keep connected to this rich source, I usually try to go back home at least once a year if I can.

Drumming is intimately related to religious rituals in Ghana. An example of this is 'Tigari', a religious occult practice of my tribe, the Ga Tribe of Nsakina. Tigari is the God of Iron and in our culture, iron is considered the most essential ingredient. Without it, we just wouldn't survive. I like to play this song with the odono, the talking drum. The odono is shaped like an hourglass and is strung with strings which the player adjusts to suit the tension of the music. Though each country has its own name for the talking drum, it's the most popular drum across West Africa.

The playing of drums was and is mainly a male-dominated activity, although some women do play in female-only drum circles. This restriction can be traced to the distinctions in society between the genders, and in particular the status of *griottes* as opposed to *griots*. Where women did play, the type of drum played was of a lesser quality and played a minor role in the music. More often they would play percussion instruments.

A present-day exception to this rule led to the formation of 'Amazones: Women Masterdrummers of Guinea' in 1998, named, as they were pioneers, after the famous women-warrior of the ancient kingdom of Dahomey (modern Benin). Mamoudou Conde, who led a world-famous group of seven male *djembe* masterdrummers called *Les Percussions de Guinée*, wanted to add women to his ensemble, but found that he faced great opposition. A descendant of the Malinke, he took his request back to the villages where the traditional ceremonies were still performed, to the elders and *griots*. Permission was granted only because Mamoudou was seen to have sufficient respect for his ancestors and their traditions. This of course reflects the enduring role which drums have in African societies, and their ritual and social significance.

Music and drumming in Jamaica

As Jamaica has many of the same kind of natural resources as are found in Africa, slaves transported there soon found ways and means to resume their ancestral practice of drumming. Some slave traders even brought African instruments to the New World along with the slaves.

Some plantation owners allowed music-making in order to settle the newly-arrived slaves. The rhythms and singing styles used in the work-songs and folksongs which developed among them are quite obviously African in origin. Later, these African musical traditions were to be fused with European forms that the slaves encountered when they were called upon to provide entertainment for their masters. The masters could be mimicked and ridiculed in the slaves' native language, or in celebrations such as Jonkunnu (see p.60).

In particular, two drumming traditions survived slavery in Jamaica. The slaves brought to Jamaica from the Gold Coast (modern Ghana) were subject to the Ashanti. These people spoke Twi, and engaged in the folk religion of Kumina (derived from two Twi words – *akom*, meaning 'to be possessed' and *ana*, meaning 'by an ancestor'). Drumming and dancing were integral parts of their daily existence whether the occasion was an illness, a celebration or a ceremony for one of the rites of passages. *Burru* drumming, too, originating in modern Ghana as a welcoming ceremony for local slaves released from captivity and returning to their communities, was revived in Jamaica. The continued existence in their purest forms of these musical traditions can be attributed to the Maroons, slaves who escaped the plantations and fled to the hills of Jamaica (see 'Historical Background', p.16).

Rastafarianism

Rastafarianism, a religious movement indigenous to Jamaica, grew out of Biblical prophecy and the teachings of Marcus Mosiah Garvey. Garvey founded the Universal Negro Improvement Association in 1914, inspiring racial pride in Black people through knowledge of their African heritage – which it was believed had been severely damaged by the experience of slavery – and advocating that Blacks all over the world should go 'back to Africa'. Although he never identified himself with the religion, he was considered a prophet. In one of his speeches, he said, 'Look to Africa for the crowning of a Black King, he shall be the Redeemer'. When, in 1930, Ras Tafari Makonen, who claimed to be a direct descendant of King David, was crowned Emperor Haile Selassie I of Ethiopia, he was seen as the Messiah.

Drumming from both these sources combined and gained prominence in Kingston, the capital of Jamaica, in the 1930s. It was soon adopted by Rastafarians in the 1950s in their *Nyabinghi* music, as the Rastafarians revered African traditions that were not altered in any way by western influences.

Nyabinghi involves drumming with at least three hand drums: a large double-sided bass drum called *thunder*, which emphasises the beat, the *funde* which maintains the rhythm, and the repeater or *akete*, which plays the melody. Other percussion is also used, including flutes. This music is played at *grounations*, or religious gatherings, and is accompanied by chanting, dancing, smoking the 'sacred herb' – ganga, praising Jah Rastafari and discussing local or world issues of importance. The famous Rastafarian reggae artist Bob Marley used *Nyabinghi* drumming and chanting in his music (listen to 'Rasta Man Chant' on his 1973 'Burnin' album). He brought worldwide publicity to both reggae music and Rastafarianism, with songs that expressed its religious and political outlook.

Social commentary, or lyrics defending particular stances or protesting against unjust situations, have been constant features in Jamaican music, as has the drum beat. At the beginning of the 20th century, Mento music did this with humorous lyrics, not unlike the Calypso songs of Trinidad, and this is still performed as a tourist attraction in Jamaica today. By the 1940s and 1950s, the influence of American big band music and rhythm and blues, produced Ska music, with its quick 'bop' beat, and accompanying 'skanking' dance move. DJs, known as toasters, spoke between each piece of music played, many of them becoming recording stars in their own right.

In the mid 1960s Ska music slowed right down and produced Rock steady with a heavy bass rhythm. It was from these roots that Reggae emerged – a fusion of traditional African rhythms, American influences and aspects that were distinctly Jamaican. With its off-beat rhythms and chanting of lyrics which came from Rastafarian religious and political beliefs, it quickly gained popularity outside Jamaica through the influence of Bob Marley and the Wailers, and Jimmy Cliff's 1973 film, *The Harder They Come*. Jamaican music continued to develop with such variations of reggae as Lovers rock and Dub, where the vocals were cut to leave a heavy bass and drum beat, allowing singers to add their own lyrics. A whole generation of performance poets in the Jamaican diaspora, such as Linton Kwesi Johnson, Micheal Smith, Benjamin Zephaniah, Jean Binta Breeze, Oku

Onouru and Mutabaruka, sprang up within this musical tradition, stirring the consciences of their audiences with serious political subject matter. And still the evolution of Reggae continues into the 21st century with the variations of Dancehall and Jungle, to name but a few: music born in the Caribbean, but with strong African roots.

Activities

- *Find out more about Rastafarians and their beliefs.*

- *Listen to different forms of Jamaican music and notice the use of drum beat and rhythms.*

From the Blues to Hip hop and Rap

The oral tradition is timeless, it is simply the tradition of passing on information orally and much of this information is handed down in the form of poems, songs and stories. People in the western world tend to see the oral tradition as something from the past and not relevant in the age of the Internet, but elsewhere the tradition carries on regardless. The oral tradition thrives when there are restrictions on people's abilities to speak or when they have no access to the media.

Benjamin Zephaniah

The oral tradition in the African diaspora of sharing stories, spreading ideas, preserving history and establishing community, and its inextricable link with music and dance, is still very much alive today, particularly in the United States of America. The field or work songs of the slaves, spirituals, the songs of the prison chain-gangs, the Blues and Jazz, are all part of one long continuum, expressing the pain of oppression and of separation, but also

signifying strength and resilience, and the comfort gained from having faith in God. Toasters, in the form of *griots*, retold the myths and legends of the community, improvising and using repetitive and often bawdy language, at every kind of social occasion and venue.

This tradition lives on in diverse forms, some of which are: schoolyard and skipping or 'double-dutch jump-rope' rhymes, the preaching and 'call and response' gospel singing in Black churches, in the work of African-American and African-Caribbean/Black British performance poets, but most notably in the African-American popular culture of Hip hop, an element of which is Rap, now emulated by young people in communities across the world.

Hip hop has four distinct elements: rapping (or MCing/emceeing), DJ-ing (incorporating mixing/cutting and scratching), breakdancing and graffiti. It is a sub-culture and art form which influences language, dress, music, thought and behaviour. Reflecting the social, political and economic conditions of young black Americans, it allows them to express themselves creatively. Rap stars are defined by their verbal dexterity and sometimes speed, their individual rhyming styles, their use of the beat of the music, and their skilful use of words and metaphors.

The origins of Rap can be clearly traced back to the late 1960s and early 1970s and reggae music. DJs working for particular record producers played the latest reggae hits at parties on their mobile sound systems and added their own vocals or toasts to the tracks. This toasting or chatting consisted of boastful and heavily-alliterated, rhyming lyrics or chants which were half-talked and half-sung. Dub music, or instrumental versions of popular songs, often the 'B' side of the vinyl record, characterised by an emphasis on the drums and a low bass, with echo and other sound effects added, provided the backdrop for the live DJ with the microphone. It also gave rise to the Dub Poet, who unlike the improvising DJ, composed his poetry in advance and then performed it with a reggae band, to music specifically composed to accompany his work. His subject matter was also different; usually commenting on the politics of the day and social injustices.

The transition from Reggae to toasting and Rapping is attributed to a DJ named Kool Herc, who moved from Kingston, Jamaica to the Bronx in New York in the early 1970s. Reggae was not popular with young New Yorkers, and increasingly neither was the commercial disco music played by the Black radio stations, so he began to perform over the instrumental and percussion breaks of the popular Funk, Disco and Soul records of the day. He realised that these sections were the best for dancing, and as they were short, he used the dub technique to extend them, using two copies of the record and an audio mixer. This also led to the development of mixing and scratching techniques and to the popularity of remixes. DJs were known to introduce themselves and greet people who attended their dances, or block parties, by 'shouting' over the instrumental breaks, using local slang terms such as 'Yo' and 'in the house', to which the crowd would respond with their own names and phrases.

Initially called emceeing, raps developed from these beginnings. Each DJ expressed his or her individual style creatively, and began to introduce rhymes and adapt them for particular audiences. Rap opened a door for young New Yorkers. As an art form it was accessible, based on verbal skill that did not need a financial investment, allowing originality and bringing the praise and

acceptance of peers. The rest is history and many rappers have gone on to become household names with glamorous lifestyles and financial fortunes. To many, Rap continues to present the illusion of a way out of poverty.

As with all genres, Rap took a commercialised route with more emphasis on the dance music and simple rhymes, but it also has developed into a sophisticated and complex form. The late 1980s saw lyrics which were much more politicised, while the 1990s brought the phenomenon of the 'gangsta' rap and rivalry between East and West coast performers which ended in deaths. Rap continues to evolve and fuse itself with other genres of popular music.

Activities

- *Explore the history of Hip hop. What kind of issues do rap artists speak about?*

- *Write your own rap on a subject you feel very strongly about.*

- *Read some of the work of Black 'performance poets' such as Linton Kwesi Johnson, Mutabaruka, Martin Glynn, Benjamin Zephaniah, Jean Binta Breeze and John Agard. Listen to recordings of their live performances. Discussion topics: What is missing from their work in print? What are the topics they have chosen to write about?*

- *Explore the differences in terminology between Reggae and Hip hop. What do the terms DJ and MC mean? Are they the same in both genres?*

- *Invite a MC, DJ or Poet to give a live performance.*

Black dance: African-Caribbean dance style

Elements of Black Dance

by community dance leader Annet Richards-Binns

- *flat feet*

- *bent knees*

- *torso forward slightly*

- *spine mobility: circular and rippling motions*

- *forward and backward movement of shoulders*

- *rippling*

- *earth-centred*

- *pelvic region: epicentre of all movement, thrusting back and forth, shaking and shimmying from side to side*

- *rhythmic movement*

Traditional African dance is an imitation of everyday life, e.g. work, animals, and generally a celebration of life. The main focus of Caribbean black dance is, however, its total lack of inhibition and its celebration of sensuality. In the Caribbean, the slaving system attempted to destroy the African culture of the slaves, which is probably the reason that in the Caribbean dance styles the surviving focus is mainly on the sensual.

In some rural areas, however, work-related rhythmic movements and songs have survived; some Afro-Caribbean dance has roots in African traditional ritual and customs, and ritualistic dances have survived in areas of Jamaica. These include the *Buru*, a fertility masquerade dance performed by women to welcome men back to the community, and the *Jonkunnu* which is performed every year at Christmastime in Jamaica (see p.60).

Other elements of African-Caribbean dance, such as are found in Calypso, Ska and Reggae are developed from the fusion of the African styles with other Caribbean dance styles. Original moves and styles developed in the Caribbean during the last 500 years, often with influences from Europe and the East, reflecting the cultural mix of this period.

The drum is the dominant musical accompaniment in African-Caribbean dance, along with singing that often involves call and response. The African-Caribbean dance is either very energetic and fast moving or it can be very slow and lazy. Whatever the mood of the dance it is to be thoroughly enjoyed.

Kumina

Kumina is the main surviving form of traditional African ritual dance that is ancestral to black people of Jamaica. As a ritual ceremony and recreational dance it came from the Congo region of West Africa where the original form known as Cumina continues to be danced. The Jamaican form retains much of the African qualities.

Kumina is practised in parts of Jamaica as a cult and for a variety of occasions: on Nine Night (see p.155), and in celebration of birth, marriage, engagements etc.

A ritual ceremony of singing, drumming, dancing and spirit possession, Kumina tends to commence at sundown and last until sun-up the next day.

In parts of Jamaica, you may see a crowd forming out of nowhere, in a town square or village corner, where a truck has pulled up with Kumina drummers and dancers. They usually wear long robes and head wraps that are definitely African in appearance. This is the sort of scene that most clearly helps to remind you of the original African heritage which is so much at the heart of Caribbean black dance styles. As you watch and listen you can see the connection coming alive in the rhythms and movements

Ska

This is Jamaican music with a corresponding dance form, that began in the late 1950s and early 1960s.

The music is a quick, lively 1-2, 1-2 drum beat accompanied by wind instruments, especially the trombone, and folk lyrics.

Dancing to Ska mainly involves swinging the arms and feet crosswise, alternating with a pulling action with the fists closed and the body bent forward almost as if miming hard work !

Numerous elements of African style can be seen in Ska. There are the African-style movements which involve the body bending forward and the use of the hips. You can also see connections between the limb-flinging movements and Black American jive/swing dance moves, which show a mixture of African and European influences.

Reggae

Reggae music emerged from the ghettos of urban Kingston in the late 1960s and spread throughout the world as an international pop music form.

The music emphasises the heavy four-beat rhythm using bass, electric guitar and drum, with a scraper coming in at the end of the measure...

Reggae rhythm is fast, chugging and tight.

Well-known reggae artists includes Bob Marley, Jimmy Cliff, Peter Tosh, Toots Hibbert, Gregory Issacs; and bands such as Black Uhuru and Third World.

Calypso

Calypso is a celebration of Caribbean life that developed mainly in Trinidad. It became established throughout the Caribbean, with its very expressive dancing to music.

Calypso can be traced to the folk songs and folk music of the Afro-West Indian slaves with their bouncy rhythms and their A-B call and response to work patterns. Calypso sounds similar to some West African music. The original *djembe* drum is used.

There are two likely origins of the name 'calypso': *kaiso* is the creole term for Calypso and is a West African cheer of approval commonly shouted during annual calypso carnival in Trinidad. Legend also has it that a man coined the name 'calypso' while singing to his lady... 'I **call** you with me **lips** press **so**'!

Soca

Soca is a combination of Soul and Calypso that developed from Calypso mainly in the 1980s. It is more contemporary than Calypso but largely derives from it. As with Calypso the comparison with modern West African music is clear, especially with Nigerian 'Highlife' music. Soca is more cosmopolitan in the Caribbean sense of the word, drawing from Jamaican reggae influences such as the DJ Toasting or rap style (see p.100), as well as from traditional Trinidad Calypso.

Caribbean folktale: Anansi stories

Anansi (alternative spelling *Anancy*), or *Kwaku Ananse* (Kwah'koo Ahnahn'sih), is a character from West African mythology, originally from the Akan people of the Ashanti state in Ghana, but now perhaps most commonly found in the Caribbean. He is a classic example of something we have seen before – the tradition that crossed the Atlantic, adopted new forms, but remained very much alive.

Anansi is the classic example of the 'trickster'. Trickster figures exist the world over and appear in the earliest oral traditions.

They generally combine many, often contradictory characteristics: semi-divinity, heroic guidance of a people, benevolent teaching, cleverness, greed, dishonesty, cruelty, and knee-slapping foolishness. The trickster is a figure of comic relief but also one in whom complete opposites struggle together within the same skin, taking turns without pattern or predictability. A people's feelings for a trickster are as varied as the trickster's own behaviour – they regard him with love, respect, gratitude, suspicion, laughter, and ridicule.

Anansi the trickster takes many forms. He can appear as a man who speaks in a high-pitched voice with a lisp, but also, most notably, as a spider. Stories passed down through the oral tradition link him with the creation of the world. His name is derived from the word *ananse*, a spider, from the Twi language of Ghana. *Ananse* also means 'Creator' in Twi, because the spider is able to make something out of nothing – his web!

Many cultures have special beings or wizards who are able to 'shapeshift', or appear in whatever form they like. On the island of Chiloé in Chile, for instance, the witches of the island are known to possess the power to transform themselves into animals. Anansi is the Twi shapeshifter, and many stories credit him with god-like powers. He is the reason why the mongoose likes to eat chicken, owls hoot, dogs fight cats, rats live in holes, lizards croak and so on.

Anansi has had quite an adventurous life, never staying still from one generation to the next. Stories about Anansi, his wife Crooky, and his son, Tacooma, travelled across the Atlantic with the people taken from West Africa as slaves to the Caribbean and the Americas, and were handed down orally from one generation to another. African-Caribbean people who emigrated to Britain in the 20th century also brought their Anansi stories with them and they are still told today.

The character and name of Anansi has changed a little along the way, in keeping with his trickster status. For example, he is sometimes crafty, cunning and treacherous, but other times very generous and full of fun. In keeping with his shapeshifting, Anansi's name has also undergone many transformations. In Africa, he was called *Kwaku* (Uncle) *Anansi*, in the Caribbean (Jamaica, Antigua, St.Vincent, Guyana, and Nevis) *Anancy* or *Nancy*. In Grenada, he is known as *Zayen*, related to the French word *araignée* – spider.

Anansi's antics are very similar to those of other animal tricksters such as *Ijapa* the tortoise in the folklore of the Yoruba people of Nigeria, who in the southern states of America became Brer Terrapin. The hare tales of the Igbo, also from Nigeria, compare with the infamous *Brer Rabbit* of North America and *Compere Lapin* (Godfather Rabbit) of Dominica, and the rabbit character in stories from St. Kitts, Trinidad, St. Lucia, Montserrat and Barbados. In Haiti the trickster tales symbolise contests between good and evil. Using song, dance and music, characters such as Papa God and the famous two-some of boastful, greedy and foolish *Uncle Bouki* and the clever, cunning *Ti Malice*, show struggles between the different impulses. However, whether hero or villain, the trickster's recognisable trait is that he nearly always manages to overcome all the trials and tribulations he faces by using his wits.

Anansi himself symbolises the triumph of wit over brute strength, something which was deeply symbolic to the slaves of the Caribbean plantations. These folk tales became a comfort to enslaved Africans, not only as something remembered from their homeland, but also as a representation of their struggles with their slave-masters. Although the slaves were the underdogs, they too were able to survive against the odds, and to maintain various elements of their cultural traditions. Even where Anansi failed, the trickster's experiences could be seen as a reflection of the setbacks that they themselves faced in their bid for freedom.

Caribbean folktales traditionally have a range of openings and closings. *Tsie na atsie* which means *Listen and hear*, is a phrase which the Akan people of Ghana use to acquire the full attention of the audience before a talk is given or a story is told. In French-speaking territories of the Caribbean, the storyteller begins by engaging in a dialogue with his audience, asking *Cric?* which means *Are you ready to listen?* and the audience calls back *Crac!* which means *Yes!*. In French-Creole, it begins with *Tim Tim*, and the response *Bois seche* (St. Lucia and Dominica), followed by *Teni...* (*There was once...*) or *Un fois...* (*Once...*), and concludes with another dialogue, *E di queek* and *Quack*. Elsewhere, the traditional English-style opening of *Once upon a time* or *There once was* is used.

The storyteller has to be a skilful performer, with the ability to take on two or three roles, utilise several different tones of voice, change pace with speed and elasticity, as well as sing at particular stages in the story.

Stories told of Anansi informed or reminded people about their history, the traditions and taboos of their society, their myths and legends, and their beliefs about life and death. They also gave everyone in the community an active connection with their African heritages, and allowed them to identify with the sufferings which they or their forebears had endured in the voyage across the Atlantic. Moreover, apart from folklore, there were stories which would tell of the good and bad deeds of ordinary folk or of those in authority. The personal identities of those concerned in the story were hidden behind the guise of animals possessing similar characteristics and temperament, something which perhaps echoed the importance of totemic animal clans in some parts of Africa.

Many Anansi stories are accompanied by songs, and end with the words, *Jack Mandora, me noh choose none*, which means *I don't take any responsibility for the story I have told*. Jack Mandora is the keeper of heaven's door, and the literal translation of *Me noh choose none* is *It's not my choice*.

Anansi stories can be exciting, educative and downright funny. There are usually lessons to learn from them. Often they highlight how you can get out of a tight corner just by using your wits. They also show that if someone tries to be too clever, greedy and ungrateful they can be taught harsh lessons.

Some stories emphasise the need to remember where you came from, where you are and how you got there in the first place. In one, Brer Anancy was helped to reach a destination since he had no means of getting there under his own steam. But when he then turned greedy and ungrateful, the odds were stacked against him.

The following excerpt from 'Anancy at Bird Cherry Island', illustrates how he was helped and then turned against those who helped him. This version was remembered by Carlton Green, who writes:

*I*T WAS *always an opportune time when a few people congregated at some leisurely place and began telling these Anancy stories. A typical time for this is when it is raining and a number of people who might be travelling take shelter in a hall, or for the older folks, in a rum bar. In the case of a big family in a home, the storyteller usually would be one of the elders. Some members would request the one they would like to hear. A favourite of mine was 'Anancy at Bird Cherry Island':*

> *Excerpt from:*
>
> ## *Anancy at Bird Cherry Island*
>
> *A FLOCK of birds were going to Bird Cherry Island where cherries were plentiful. They were to fly from the mainland across waters to reach the Island. Having wings this was no problem for them.*
>
> *Brer Anancy also wanted to go, but having no feathers and wings to fly there with the birds, it was impossible for him. Using his wits he befriended the birds and asked each of them to lend him a feather-wings so that he could join them on that flight.*
>
> *The birds gave him feather-wings so that he could fly. Having got there, Brer Anancy became greedy. Every cherry tree the birds flew into, Brer Anancy claimed that his grandfather left them for him and the birds should not feed from them.*
>
> *Brer Anancy claimed every tree, leaving the birds with none to feed from. Remembering that they gave him feather-wings to get there, they got angry and took back their feather-wings. Having been left with no wings to fly across the waters to reach home on the mainland, he had to find another way home.*
>
> *However, his wit kicked in again, and he eventually did find a way home, but not before he conned brother alligator who rescued him from drowning in the water, after he jumped in and could not swim.*

Anansi and Common Sense

Anansi's Pot of Wisdom – African Version

KWAKU ANANSI regarded himself as the wisest of all creatures. He knew how to build bridges, to make dams and roads, to weave, and to hunt. But he didn't wish to share this wisdom with other creatures. He decided one day that he would gather together all the wisdom of the world and keep it for himself. So he went around collecting wisdom, and each bit he found he put in a large earthen pot. When the pot was full, Anansi prepared to carry it into a high tree top where no one else could find it. He held the pot in front of him and began to climb.

Anansi's son Intikuma was curious about what his father was doing, and he watched from behind some bushes. He saw Anansi holding the pot in front of him against his stomach. He saw that this made it hard for Anansi to grasp the tree he was climbing. At last he couldn't keep quiet any longer and he said, 'Father, may I make a suggestion?'

Anansi was startled and angry, and he shouted, 'Why are you spying on me?'

Intikuma replied, 'I only wanted to help you.'

Anansi said, 'Is this your affair?'

Intikuma said to him, 'It's only that I see you are having difficulty. When you climb a tree, it is very hard to hold a pot in front. If you put the pot on your back, you can climb easily.'

Anansi tried it. He took the pot from in front and put it on his back. He climbed swiftly. But then he stopped. He looked at Intikuma and was embarrassed, for although he carried so much wisdom in the pot, he had not known how to climb with it.

In anger, Kwaku Anansi took the pot and threw it from the tree top. It fell on the earth and shattered into many pieces. The wisdom that was in it scattered in all directions. When people heard what had happened, they came and took some of the wisdom Anansi had thrown away. And so today, wisdom is not all in one place. It is everywhere. Should you find a foolish man, he is one who didn't come when the others did to take a share of the wisdom.

This is the story the Ashanti people are thinking of when they say: 'One head can't go into consultation.'

Anancy an Common-Sense – Jamaican Version[6]

ONCE UPON a time Anancy tink to himself seh dat if him coulda collect all de common-sense ina de worl an keep it fi himself, den him boun to get plenty money an plenty powah, for everybody would haffi come to him wid dem worries an him woulda charge dem very dear wen him advise dem.

Anancy start fi collect up an collect up all de common-sense him coulda fine an put dem ina one big-big calabash. Wen him search an search an couldn't fine no more common-sense Anancy decide fi hide him calabash full a common-sense pon de top of a high-high tree which part nobody else coulda reach it.

So Anancy tie a rope roun de neck a de calabash an tie de two end a de rope togedda, an tie de rope roun him neck so da de calabash wasa res pon him belly. Anancy star fi climb up de high-high tree, which part him was gwine hide de calabash, but him couldn't climb too good nor too fas for de calabash wasa get in him way everytime him try fi climb. Anancy try an try so till all of a sudden him hear a voice buss out a laugh backa him, an wen him look him see lickle bwoy a stan up a de tree root a laugh an halla seh: 'Wat a foo-fool man! If yuh want to climb de tree front way, why yuh don't put de calabash behine yuh?'

Well sah, Anancy soh bex fi hear dat big piece a common-sense come outa de mout in such a lickle bit of bwoy afta him did tink dat him did collect all de common-sense in de worl, dat Anancy grab off de calabash from roun him neck an fling it dung a de tree root, an de calabash bruck up in minces an de common-sense dem scatter out ina de breeze all ovah de worl an everybody get a lickle bit a common-sense. Is Anancy meck it.

Jack Mandora, me noh choose none.

Terrapin's Pot of Sense – American Version

*I*N THE OLD *days they was a big competition 'mongst the animals to see which of 'em could collect the most good sense. Buh Coon, Buh Fox, Buh Guinea, Buh Geese, Buh Snake, and all the others went running' around pickin' up pieces of good sense on the ground or on the bushes or wherever they could find 'em. Buh Coon had a little pile of good sense in his place, Buh Rabbit had a little pile in his place, Buh Rooster had some in his place. Of course, they was all in such a hurry to outdo the other folks that some of the sense they picked up wasn't so good, and some was downright spoiled. But everyone was braggin' 'bout what a pile of sense he had back home. Trouble was, the places they had to keep it wasn't just right. Buh Possum's house had a leak in the roof, and everytime it rained, the water came drip, drip, drip, down on Possum's pile of sense. Buh 'Gator he put his sense in the nest where he keep his eggs, but every time the young ones hatch out they jump around and kicked the good sense all over the place. Buh Rooster have his good sense in a nice pretty pile, but his wife, Sister Hen she's so nearsighted she can't tell sense from corn, and she was always a-peckin' at it. Buh Duck he want to fly South in the winter and don't know what to do with his pile of sense.*

Well, Buh Terrapin, he got a fine idea. He say, 'Friends, what we need is a caretaker to take care of all the sense we gathered. You just bring it to me and I'll be the caretaker.'

All the animals liked that idea, 'cause it eased their worries for 'em. So they all brought the sense they'd collected to Buh Terrapin, and he gave each and everyone of 'em a receipt for it. Then he took all that sense and put it in a big iron cookin' pot.

Afterward he begin to study where could he hang the pot. At last he decided he goin' to hang it top of a great big sycamore tree safe and

sound. So he took the pot in front of him and went to climb the tree with it. But he got a powerful problem, 'cause the pot was pretty big and Terrapin's legs was too short in the first place to be climbin' trees. Took Terrapin most of the day to get halfway up. All the critters was standin' around watchin' that pot of sense go up, sayin', 'Hey there, Buh Terrapin, careful of that pot! It got my sense in it!'

Just afore nightfall a wind come up and begin blowin' things around. The top of the sycamore tree began to switch back and forth. Wind got stronger, and the top of the tree commence to whippin' around till Buh Terrapin couldn't hold on no more. He hollered, 'Here I come!' and let go.

Buh Terrapin landed smack on his back and lay right there where he fall. The iron pot hit the ground and rolled this way and that. Naturally, everything that was in it got scattered all over. All the critters started to run around pickin' up pieces of sense. Everything was mixed up, and couldn't no one tell which was his and which was somebody's else's. Didn't have time then to figure out what was good sense, or ordinary sense, or plain stupidity – everybody just grabbed.

And when they had they hands full and didn't know what to do with it, Buh Horse say, 'I don't know what all you folks doin' with yours, but I'm puttin' mine in my head.' And when he did that, the others say, 'I'm puttin' mine in my head too,' and they did the same as Buh Horse did. That's how come all the critters got sense in their heads. And they got good sense and bad sense as well. Some's luckier than others in what they picked up. Most everybody got a mixture through.

When that part of it was all over, they saw Buh Terrapin still on his back, and they righted him. They saw his shell was all cracked from fallin' on the ground, just the way it's been ever since. They went away and left him. Terrapin he crawled around in the grass lookin' for bits of sense they'd left behind. He found some, but they hadn't left much for him. When you see Buh Terrapin crawlin' around in the grass nowadays you can figure he's still lookin' for some scraps of sense.

That's a sad story for Buh Terrapin, ain't it? But some folks figure he had it comin' on account of they think he was fixin' to get all the sense for himself by appointin' himself caretaker.

Activities

- Compare the three versions of the same Anansi story. List the similarities and differences.

- Draw a picture of Anansi, showing him to be part spider, part man.

- Write your own Anansi story. Let there be a moral to your tale!

Anancy

Anancy is a spider;
Anancy is a man;
Anancy's West Indian
And West African.

Sometimes, he wears a waistcoat;
Sometimes, he carries a cane;
Sometimes, he sports a top hat;
Sometimes, he's just plain,
Ordinary, black, hairy spider.

Anancy is vastly cunning,
Tremendously greedy,
Excessively charming,
Hopelessly dishonest,
Warmly loving,
Firmly confident,
Fiercely wild,
A fabulous character,
Completely out of our mind
And out of his too.

Anancy is a master planner,
A great user
Of other people's plans;
He pockets everybody's food,
Shelter, land, money, and more;
He achieves mountains of things,
Like stolen flour dumplings;
He deceives millions of people,
Even the man in the moon;
And he solves all the mysteries
On earth, in air, under sea.

And always,
Anancy changes
From a spider into a man
And from a man into a spider
And back again
At the drop of a sleepy eyelid.

Andrew Salkey

Anancy the Spiderman[7]

Anancy is a spider, Anancy is a man,
Anancy is West Indian an West African.
Anancy sailed to Englan on a banana boat,
An when he got to Brixton, everybody gave a
  shout.

Anancy! Anancy!
Anancy the magic spiderman.
Anancy! Anancy!

Anancy an Brer Englishman.
Anancy! Anancy!
Anancy the magic spiderman.
Anancy! Anancy!
Anancy an Brer Englishman.

Anancy is a jiver, he's frisky as a fly.
A shifty plastic being, an that is no lie.
Anancy is a trickster, he's sensitive to guile,
He sometimes can be like a very greedy chile.

Proverbs

A wise man who knows proverbs can settle disputes

Yoruba

It is believed that proverbs are more popular in Africa than in any other part of the world, as is the love of speaking in symbolic terms. Proverbs contain the wisdom of African communities, condensing in poetic form the whole spectrum of human experience. All proverbs have a message for the listener and their intention is to pass on the traditions and moral codes of the community.

Proverbs also have an important social function within many African societies. Amongst the Yoruba of Nigeria, there is a set of established proverbs which only the elders are allowed to utter. Others in the community must use 'imitation proverbs', and have to apologise if they accidentally use a proverbial expression when speaking to an elder. In some African societies, the proverb is such an integral feature that it would be virtually impossible for any kind of negotiation to take place without one being used.

Some proverbs are not easily understood outside of their context, but give great insights into the ways of life and thinking of the society from which they originated. Others, however, are simple and clear, requiring no explanation, and are universal in their teaching matter. Some, relating to universals in human nature, are almost identical to those found elsewhere in the world.

African proverbs are so diverse that they appear not only in word form, but can also be found woven into cloth. One particular example of this is the *Kente* pattern, *Tikoro nko agyina – One head does not go into council (Two heads are better than one)*, which was presented by the Republic of Ghana to the United Nations, and can be seen in the United Nations Building in New York City.

The connections between Africa, the Caribbean and the Americas are also very evident in proverbs.

The disease which affects the eyes usually affects the nose as well

Yoruba, Nigeria

What hurt eyes does make nose run

Trinidad

Tales are the food of the ear

Igbo, Nigeria

Talk is the ear's food

Jamaica

The rain does not recognise anyone as a friend
Whoever it sees it drenches

Yoruba, Nigeria

It rains and everyman feels it someday

Black American

A man has to wait a long time to find a hyena playing a guitar

Wolof, Senegal

Haitian Proverbs

Mwen ba w sal w ap mande salon
I give you a room and now you want my
living room

Bouch manje tout manje, men li pa pale
tout pawòl
The mouth may eat any food but should
not speak on any subject
(Discretion is important)

Yon sèl dwèt pa mange kalalou
You cannot eat okra with one finger
(We must all cooperate)

American South (African-American Proverbs

Jest countin' stumps don't clear the field

Talkin' 'bout fire doesn't boil the pot

Hand plow can't make furrows by itself

Death don't see no difference 'tween the
big house and the cabin

Old Used-to-Do-It-This-Way don't help
none today

Storyteller Jane Grell writes:

I WAS BORN *and grew up on the island of Dominica, not to be confused with the Dominican Republic. There, the official language is English and the folk language French Creole or Kwéyol as it is now called. There was no electricity in my village during my early childhood, and so moonlit evenings were magical. People stayed up much later than usual. We roasted corn-on-the-cob on coal-pots, cooked breadnuts (similar to chestnuts), played hide-and-seek and ring games. The highlight of those evenings were the contes and tim-tims (tales and riddles).*

The storyteller would call out:	*Tim-tim! (I'll give you a riddle)*
The audience would respond:	*Bwa sesh! (Go on then)*
Storyteller:	*D'lo dubut! (standing water)*
Audience:	*kann! (sugar cane)*
Storyteller:	*D'lo sispanne! (hanging water!)*
Audience:	*koko! (coconut!)*

Featuring as part of the contes and tim-tim sessions were proverbs. Many of them were actually used in everyday speech. Here are some examples:

Chatte pas la, watte ka baye bal	*(When the cats are away, the mice play)*
La lin kouwi, jou badine y	*(The moon runs as day overtakes her)*
La fime pas ka sorti sans dife	*(No smoke without fire)*
Dans ka wi kors	*(Fools laugh at themselves)*
Tete pas jamais tot lou pou l'estomac	*(A mother can always feed her many children)*

English-speaking Caribbean

Jamaica
Bermuda
The Bahamas
The Cayman Islands
Antigua and Barbuda
St. Kitts and Nevis

Turks and Caicos
St. Vincent and the Grenadines
Trinidad and Tobago
Guyana
U.S. Virgin Islands
British Virgin Islands
Grenada

Belize
St. Lucia
Anguilla
Dominica
Barbados
Montserrat

Spanish-speaking Caribbean

Cuba
Dominican Republic
Puerto Rico

French-speaking Caribbean

Haiti
French Guiana
Guadaloupe
Martinique

Dutch-speaking Caribbean

Suriname
Curacao

Aruba
Bonaire
St. Eustatius

St. Maarten
Saba

Proverbs also reveal something of the historical experiences of the societies in which they are found. Caribbean proverbs, when compared with proverbs from other parts of the world, tend to be very negative in their form, meaning and context. Over three quarters of them contain a negative word such as no, never or nothing, and over half of the rest include words with negative meanings such as kill, lose, break; and most of the remainder are warnings or advice against doing something. Though most definitely resulting from wisdom and experience, they are seldom presented in a positive way. It is difficult not to see this as deriving from the negative historical experiences of people of African origin in the Caribbean.

If you don't hear, you will feel

What is done in the dark will appear in the light

One finger can't catch flea

Don't hang yuh hat higher than you can reach

Drummer can't dance

No rain, no rainbow

Hurry – hurry mek bad curry

Mouth open, story jump out

Don't call alligator long-mouth till you cross river

Activity

- *Choose a few of either the African or Caribbean proverbs and write an English version.*

Carnival

Historians have traced the origins of Carnival back to the ancient-Roman festival of Saturn, Saturnalia, and the medieval European 'Feast of Fools'. Such festivities usually involved wild huge parties, with much eating, drinking and general merry-making. It was everyone's social duty to have a good time. All social distinctions were turned upside down, with wealthy people dressing and acting like poor people and vice versa. Masks were worn to hide an individual's identity, and for a time people abandoned their normal and polite ways of behaving.

This celebration was frowned upon following the rise of Christianity, but such was its appeal among the masses that it was adopted by the Christian calendar, and two days of feasting and celebration were allowed before the beginning of Lent.

Centuries later this Carnival tradition had spread right across Europe in countries such as Italy, Spain, France, Portugal, parts of Poland and Germany, and many strongly Catholic areas. As European countries colonised the Caribbean and the Americas, and involved themselves in the slave trade, the tradition of Carnival became fused with the African tradition of masquerade. Carnival became increasingly international, spreading to Haiti, Trinidad, Brazil and other areas of the Caribbean and to New Orleans in the USA. It has migrated still further with African and African-Caribbean peoples who have settled in large cities all over the USA and Canada.

The styles of carnival are as many as the places where they are celebrated. The carnival in Bahía, Brazil, is known to be one of the most authentic mixtures of Yoruba and European traditions – although Rio de Janeiro beats Bahía for glitz and pizzazz. In New Orleans, Louisiana, the Mardi Gras has resulted from the mix of French settlers with African-Americans and Native Americans. In Canada, Trinidadian emigrants have held their Caribana every August in Toronto, since 1967. Britain also has a very popular and well-established annual celebration, held in Notting Hill in London on August bank holiday weekend, with smaller versions around the country in cities such as Bristol (St. Paul's) in July.

Modern carnival has incorporated the ancient African traditions of parading and of 'circling', moving in circles through villages, dressed in costumes and wearing masks; the circling of villages was meant to bring good fortune, healing and settling angry ancestors in the next world. Moreover, the creation today of masks and costumes by mixing a range of natural objects and materials – fabric, shells, grass, bones, beads and feathers – is also an idea borrowed from African tradition, where these items were used to represent individual spirits or concepts. For example, feathers were used as a symbol of our ability to rise above earthly problems and be transported to another world, where we can be spiritually reborn.

Many argue that Trinidad celebrates Carnival at its best. In this small country, which is made up of a wide range of peoples originating from all over the globe (in particular Africa, India, France, Spain and China), each with their own beliefs and traditions, Carnival is an opportunity for everyone to unite and celebrate for three days each year. The Trinidadian Carnival is preceded by many days of pre-Carnival events which are just as exciting and engaging as the three main days. In February or March each year, on the Sunday, Monday and Tuesday immediately before the beginning of Lent, it attracts people from all over the world, who come to watch the parades of masqueraders, listen to the steel bands and calypso singers, and join in the singing and dancing in the streets.

In Trinidad, the celebration of Carnival is believed to date back to 1783, when French Catholic immigrants arrived on the island. They brought with them their tradition of fancy masked balls, with beautiful costumes and wigs. There were concerts and processions by torchlight. Elaborately decorated carriages paraded through the streets and showered onlookers with confetti. There was much silliness. People disguised themselves – even as slaves – and paid surprise visits to their neighbours.

At first the slaves were not allowed to take part in these events. They watched, and soon began to imitate, adding aspects of their own folklore and rituals and thus creating their own version of Carnival (see 'Jonkunnu', p.60). Music and dance from their own tradition, in the form of drum rhythms, stick fighters, stilt dancers and large puppets were added to transform the nature of the original celebration. Later on, however, slaves were encouraged to take part as a means of introducing them to the Roman Catholic religion, rather than holding on to their own customs and forms of worship.

To the Africans working on the plantations, the new Carnival became a way of expressing themselves and holding on to their culture under the disguise of a European celebration, and so of mocking their masters. After Emancipation in 1834, when the freed slaves were allowed to have their own Carnivals in the streets, the celebrations became much more elaborate and bettered the masked balls in popularity.

These early street Carnivals held by the newly-freed slaves were much more reminiscent of their traditional African celebrations, with activities such as stick-fighting. Europeans found this very violent and alarming, and so alienated themselves from these celebrations, later bringing in laws to restrict them. However, such restrictions led to the creation of new art forms which transformed the Trinidadian Carnival (see 'Steel bands' p.122).

Denise Taitt: Carnival in Trinidad

*G*ROWING UP *in Trinidad was truly a magical experience for me and my most treasured memories come from that time. When I reflect on my childhood, scenes of sunshine flood my mind, taking me back to a time where games such as marbles, hopscotch and cricket filled the streets, and cars gave way to children playing. Climbing trees and playing on the beach are logged too, with the sweet-tasting juice of sugar cane and mangoes, peppery hot roti all blended together with singing and dancing and storytelling – tales told by the elders depicting events of a long time past which intrigued and frightened you, but held you spellbound, afraid to move, afraid to breathe: and then came the laughter, the big belly laughter which made you feel safe again.*

But the best memory of them all is CARNIVAL. Now Carnival in Trinidad is no ordinary affair, it's not one of these village affairs you have here in England. And if you think Notting Hill Carnival in big, well you ain't seen nothing yet! Let me tell you, the whole of Trinidad, every man, woman and child can't wait for Carnival. Planning and preparation for Carnival happens months in advance and when it comes you are partying and celebrating for two days. Now Carnival tells the story of the Caribbean, drawing on historical links with Africa and India and is always celebrated on the Monday and Tuesday before Lent, so you know people are partying hard.

My earliest memories of Carnival have me running and hiding with fright. Picture the scene, Monday, Jouvert Day, the day you pay the devil and the devil is coming to collect. Men dressed in ragged shorts, painted black all over and chanting as they beat a haunting rhythm on an old tin can with a stick, running through the streets in every town and every village, collecting the support of every dog they encounter, whose barks add to the haunting as they sing – 'Pay the devil jab jab I want money, pay the devil jab jab I want money, I black like hell, and I come from hell, pay the devil jab jab I want money' – over and over. If caught, you paid to avoid being marked, but so strong was my fear of these men that I would run, tears streaming from my eyes, trying to get home as fast as I could to hide under my bed. I felt sure they were true devils and I would be taken away taken to hell, never to see my family again.

That was all part of the fun to build up your senses and your excitement for the real 'ting', Carnival Tuesday, when the streets were again filled with music, sweet melodic tunes of skilled pan-men beating tunes to set your feet jumping, hips shaking and your hands waving in the air. Masqueraders dressed up in costumes made of feathers, silk, velvet, and colours, like the rainbow, red yellow, blue, green streaming down the road on and on. Soldiers, sailors, birds, spiders, skeleton shapes, some big, some small, creative and outlandish costumes tell their tales. And if you weren't part of a band, you still partied, jumping, prancing and dancing – the whole street the whole village, the whole town, the whole Island. 'That is magic – that is CARNIVAL!'

Preparations for Carnival actually begin soon after the previous Carnival is over, but start in earnest immediately after Christmas. Creative teams organise themselves in *Mas Camps*. Costumes and three-dimensional 'dancing mobiles' have to be designed and made, with methods including papier-maché and the binding, bending, welding, sewing and glueing of a host of materials, such as bamboo, wire, netting, foam, paint, bright materials, feathers, sequins, foil and glitter. Calypsos have to be written and rehearsed, and the steel bands have to practise for all of the competitions ahead. Firstly, there are the 'Prelims', when the preliminary rounds of the competitions take place, and prizes are awarded to the best entries in each category: King and Queen of Carnival, Calypso Monarch, Best Steel Band, and Band of the Year. There is also a Junior (children's) Carnival. Following on from these weeks of pre-Carnival activities, there are three main days of Carnival:

Carnival Sunday, or Dimanche Gras (Fat Sunday)

On this day people gather in the capital, Port of Spain, and other main towns and villages throughout Trinidad and Tobago. It is a day for meeting friends and going to parties and dances. Some of these events go on until the early hours of the Monday morning, when at 4am. Carnival is officially declared open by the President and the firing of a rocket in the capital.

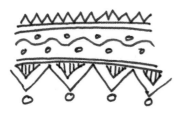

Carnival Monday, or Jour Ouvert
(or 'J'Ouvert' as Trinidadians call it – meaning 'Open Day' in French)

This is the official opening day, 'break of day', of the street festival. Traffic is restricted and the morning begins with 'jump up'; people, often in simple, home-made costumes, dancing, jumping or shuffling along in the streets to music provided by steel bands, moving slowly as in a samba. This is also when the traditional characters and costumes of Carnival, *Ol' Mas*, are paraded. As many of the participants have been up all night, there is a rest in the mid-morning or afternoon, and the 'jumping' and processions start again later and go on well into the next morning. Stalls are set up along the roadside offering sweet and spicy (mainly East Indian) snacks and drinks, including rum and other spirits mixed with coconut water, *mauby* and sorrel, to keep the party-goers going.

Carnival Tuesday, or Mardi Gras

The festival reaches its climax on this day with great parades through the streets of the *Mas Bands*, large troupes of masqueraders, often in their hundreds, in impressive themed costumes, dancing to the sounds of their own musicians. Onlookers join in the dancing and excitement. In the capital, the revellers end their parade in Queen's Park Savannah, where the judging of the many competitions is held.

Carnival enters its *Las Lap* as darkness falls on Tuesday evening, and ends quite abruptly at midnight, when Ash Wednesday begins.

Some traditional Ol' Mas characters

Jab Molassi (Molasses Devil), Devil or Jab Jabs

Presumably from the French for devil (*diable*), this character is present in most Carnivals around the world. He was often covered in soot and molasses, now black or blue paint, and threatened the audience to smear their clothes with the same unless he was paid not to. As molasses are produced from sugar cane which was grown by the slaves on the plantations, this figure is seen as a symbol of slavery.

Borokit or Burroquites

This character, whose name is related to the Spanish for 'little donkey', is composed of the head of a horse or donkey worn over a long skirt with a bamboo frame underneath. The wearer of this costume holds reins in his/her hands and appears to ride the animal. It is thought that this either represents Spanish bull-fighting or a religious Hindu ritual.

Canboulay

From the term *cannes brulees* or burning cane this group, dressed as slaves, is a reminder of the burning of the stubble on a sugar plantation. Slaves from neighbouring plantations were often brought in to help put out the fires. They parade singing, drumming and carrying burning torches, and are subjected to mock beatings.

Dame Lorraine

This character is a ridiculously exaggerated
aristocratic lady.

Moco/Mocko Jumbie

A tall figure, dancing on stilts, dressed in a
long skirt and a brightly coloured satin or
velvet jacket, wearing an Admiral's hat
decorated with feathers.

The origins of this character can be traced as
far back as the 13th century, although it
could be much earlier, and is found in many
West African countries, such as Ghana,
Nigeria, Gambia, Togo, Benin, Sierra Leone,
Senegal and Ivory Coast. The height of

Mocko Jumbie, sometimes as much as 10 – 20 feet, is a symbol of the power and greatness of God. These characters are seen as the protectors of villages, able to see evil spirits approaching and thus warn the villagers. Their supernatural powers can ward off evil spirits. Mocko Jumbies played an important role in many West African religious ceremonies, in particular the rites of passage when boys became men and girls became women. Many, particularly children, found them frightening because of their height. They were often played by someone from the village, but would remain anonymous, wearing a mask made of goat skin, decorated with cowrie shells. Their outfit also had mirrors, as evil spirits were afraid of viewing themselves.

Also featured in traditional Carnival processions were military bands dressed as soldiers or sailors engaged in mock battles, and wild Indians, a reminder of the indigenous inhabitants of the Americas – but later changed to look more like the 'Red Indians' or Native Americans in Western films. There were also jesters, clowns, minstrels, pierrots, robbers, pirates, doctors and a variety of other professions.

Carnival music

Steel bands

Drumming, along with other forms of cultural expression amongst the African slaves, was restricted and later banned. In Trinidad, drumming was banned in the 1880s and riots followed. In consequence, new and 'acceptable' percussion instruments were devised, which could retain the rhythmic elements of drumming. The first of these were *tamboo bamboo* (from the French word *tambour* meaning drum), made from the readily available bamboo. Varying lengths of bamboo tubes were cut, hollowed out, dried and tuned, the largest of which, the 'boom' or 'base', were stomped on the ground by the bands as they marched in the carnival procession. There was also the *foule*, two smaller sticks which were held one in each hand and struck together, end to end; and the *cutter*, which was a thin stick worn across the shoulder and beaten with a piece of wood. Other 'instruments' such as bottles and spoons, dustbin lid drums and graters scraped with a piece of metal, added to the array of sound-making.

However, this form of music too was found to be unacceptable by the government, because of the noise and fear of riots, and was banned in the 1920s. The first 'pans' were formed by the crafting of such items as biscuit tins and dustbin lids into instruments, and these metallic instruments were played in what were called 'iron' or 'pan' bands. It was not long before it was realised that if these metal items were beaten, they could be transformed from non-pitched to pitched instruments. The first steel drums were small convex, metal containers, which were carried in one hand and beaten by the other, and were not very tuneful. During and after the World War Two, oil drums discarded by the Americans were identified as having great potential for the development of the steel pan. By the 1950s the style and tuning had improved, and by the time of Independence in 1962 the steel band was officially recognised and given respectability, and the new government encouraged big businesses to sponsor bands. Carnival became the highlight of the year for the bands, thus giving rise to the strong competitive spirit that prevails today.

To play in a steel band you do not have to read music, but just have an 'ear' for a tune. A full steel band, or *orchestra*, consists of four sections: the Front, the Middle, the Back and the Rhythm section, but smaller bands are more than capable of playing popular tunes.

Calypso

Another essential component part of Carnival is the Calypso, again originating in Trinidad, but with an African heritage. A Calypso is a song specially composed for the event, with a topical theme. It is usually set to a catchy tune, but this is not as important as the words, which are cleverly put together. They are often humorous to the point of being insulting, and often ridicule or criticise local, national or international events, scandals, personalities, or social or political issues. In Trinidad, the Calypso has been known to wield sufficient power to unseat a politician, with a Carnival song highlighting a particular wrongdoing.

'Education is a must' by Slinger Francisco, The Mighty Sparrow, Calypso King of the World published by Sparrow Music

Education is a must

Education, education, this is the foundation
Our rising population needs sound education
You'll recognize anywhere you go
Have your certificate to show
To enjoy any kind of happiness
Knowledge is the key to success

Children go to school and learn well
Otherwise later on in life you go ketch real hell
Without education in your head
Your whole life will be pure misery you better off dead
For there is simply no room in this whole wide world
For an uneducated little boy or girl
Don't allow idle companions to lead you astray
To earn tomorrow you got to learn today

For employment, yes employment,
You must be intelligent
So it's essential, very essential
To have your credentials
But if you blockedheaded like a mule
Just remember, no one will employ a fool
You will be the last one to be hired
And the first one to be fired

Illiteracy, illiteracy is man's greatest enemy
It's your duty, yes your duty
To stamp it out completely
Ignorance always impedes progress
Education saves you much distress
So learn, learn, learn as much as you can
For the nation's future is in your hand.

It's a treasure, yes a treasure beyond any measure
Just secure, just secure it
Don't ever ignore it
To fight life's battles come what may
Education lights your way
Without it you'll never get through
Success or failure now is up to you

The following was written as a result of the scandalous event of the abdication of King Edward VIII in 1936 to marry Mrs Wallis Simpson, an American divorcee.

Edward VIII – Love, Love Alone

The Duke of Iron:	*Now, it's love, love alone* *That cause King Edward to leave his throne*

Chorus:	*It's love, love alone* *The cause King Edward to leave his throne*

The Duke of Iron:	*Yes, we know Edward is noble and great* *But love will cause him to abdicate*

Oh, what a sad disappointment
Was endured by the British government

On the 10th of December, we heard the talk
That he gave the throne to the Duke of York

He said, 'I'm sorry my mother is going to grieve
But I cannot help, I am bound to leave'

Yes, we got the money, we got the talk
And the fancy walk to just to suit New York

'And if I can't get a boat to set me free
Well, I will walk to Miss Simpson across the sea

Scepter, robes and my crown is on my mind
But I cannot leave Miss Simpson behind'

Lord Invader:	*And if you see Miss Simpson walk in the street* *She can fall an angel with her body beat*

Oh, how Baldwin tried to break down his plan
He said, 'Come what may the American'

The Duke of Iron:	*'Yea, they can take my crown, they can take my throne* *But they must leave Miss Simpson and me alone'*

Oh, let the organ roll, let the church bell ring
Good luck to our second bachelor king

Lord Invader:	*Though he is gone, don't give him bad name* *For you and I might have done the same*
Macbeth the Great:	*Aspersion on Simpson, they try to cast* *They even said that she had a shady past*
The Duke of Iron:	*Now on the annals of history* *He has left a record for intensity*

Rufus Callender (Caresser)

Sound systems

These large indoor or open-air dances, with DJs playing the tunes through huge speaker boxes, with deafening bass lines, have become another common feature of Carnival.

Activities

- *Find out about the history of Notting Hill Carnival and the role played in its development by people such as Claudia Jones and Alex Pascall.*

- *Listen to Calypso music. Research famous Calypsos, which have stood the test of time. What were their themes?*

- *Individually or in a group, compose your own Calypso about a famous event, person or everyday situation that interests you, or that most people can relate to. Remember to give it a catchy tune and rhythm, so that it can be easily remembered. It should have four verses, each with eight lines, and a chorus that is repeated between each verse. Try to make it funny, or with a clever play on words that makes fun of, or criticises your subject. Each individual or group can then perform their Calypso to the others. Why not hold a competition to find the best Calypso King, or Queen, or Band?*

- *Consider creating a steel band in your school or group. Organise fundraising events to cover the costs of the pans, tuition and outfits. Use the internet to find a steel pan-maker and tutor in your area.*

Section Four

Rites of Passage

I am because we are and because we are therefore I am.

John Mbiti

Rites of passage are rituals marking the transition from one stage of the human cycle to another, such as birth, growing up, marriage and death. These rituals create a sense of belonging, of acceptance, and mark a new beginning as an individual is initiated into the next phase of his or her life.

In Africa these milestones are part of the individual's ongoing participation in the community. People need a certain type of knowledge and wisdom to participate as responsible adults in African society, and the acquisition of this knowledge is not left to chance. Rites of passage, inextricably linking individual and society, are celebrated with great reverence and respect in the form of initiation ceremony traditions established many centuries earlier by the community's ancestors. The rites are deeply rooted in African religious beliefs, with highly detailed daily practices that protect and strengthen the community, and are accompanied by specific masquerades, dances and foods.

In many ways, then, this part of the book brings together aspects which we have touched on before to show how African-Caribbean culture must be viewed as a whole body of belief, practice and identity. Masquerades are both part of the oral tradition and part of a rite of passage; food has both a position in its own right within the culture, and a ritualistic purpose; dance is a joyous celebration in its own right, but it also has wider significance.

In Africa, the process of initiation into society begins before a child is even born. In many African cultures it is believed that children come from the spirit world, and that each of them arrives with a unique, God-given purpose, in the form of talents or gifts that will benefit the community. The name given to a child will often indicate the contribution the child is destined to make, and therefore is carefully chosen. And it is the responsibility of the whole community to ensure that the individual fulfils his or her pre-determined role in society.

The move from childhood into adulthood is also a period marked with ritual, usually involving a time of withdrawal from the community for instruction, and the endurance of a painful experience or one requiring bravery. Circumcision is the central rite of passage for boys. For girls, initiation ceremonies mark their entry into adulthood and announce to the community that they are eligible for marriage; great emphasis is placed upon preparing them to be good wives and mothers.

Marriage and parenthood are also viewed as important aspects of the cycle of life. A marriage brings two families or kinship groups together, although the two being married are also of course joined as individuals. As with other areas of life in Africa the focus is on wider family and community rather than the individual. Adulthood is not considered to be fully achieved until a person is married and has children. When marriages produce children, the central point of the life cycle is reached, and the whole spectrum of the community meets: the dead, the living and the not yet born (see 'Death and ancesterhood', p.150).

Once the children of a couple have been raised and become fully integrated members of the community, parents move on to the position which has the highest status in African society, that of 'elders'. More than just an 'older' person in the community, elders have lived a purposeful life. They are respected for their wisdom and the fact that they represent tradition. Having passed through all the previous initiation rites successfully, they are considered to be exemplary role models for other members of society.

An extension of the importance of age in African societies is ancestorhood. This comes after the death of an elder, when they pass over into the spirit world, taking with them the status they achieved while living. Unlike many other societies in the world, in which it is a taboo topic of conversation and generally feared, in African society death is accepted as a natural part of the rhythm of life. It is not an ending. If a life has been lived to the fullest extent, fulfilling its destined journey from the goals given at birth, the individual moves into the revered position of an ancestor. Successfully passing through all of these rites of passage is the process by which this ideal life and, subsequently ancestorhood, can be attained.

An Ashanti folktale illustrates the belief in death as a natural part of the cycle of life. It tells of how death came to be:

THERE WAS a time when there was no death, and when people used to live forever. Because there were no deaths, there were also no births. However, the people were interested in knowing about bearing children and asked the gods if they could have children. The gods refused, but the people kept pleading and begging until the gods gave in. They were allowed on one condition, that with every birth there must be a death. And the people agreed.

John Mbiti

For the last few decades there has been a growing interest in the revival of African-centred rites of passage among peoples of African origin in the diaspora, especially in the United States of America. It is perceived that the absence of rites of passage within communities has led to generations of people losing their way. Blame for wayward children with no respect or ambition, broken marriages, dysfunctional and distant families, lack of respect for the elderly, and general lack of community spirit, is assigned to the loss of direction, purpose and guidance that these rites provide. This is why, in addition to European-style celebrations of the various stages in the life cycle, many Black people of African origin are returning to their 'roots' and embracing 're-invented' traditional African initiation ceremonies.

In the USA and the Caribbean, Rites of Passage (ROP) programmes have sprung up in great abundance, as part of community and church programmes. Events such as 'naming ceremonies' and 'jumping the broom' are becoming commonplace, and are incorporated into their modern counterparts, christening and marriage services. Thirteenth birthday celebrations, too, are very popular. Following a year-long preparation period, the celebration involves young people presenting the results of a project centred around an interest they have, which they have worked on with a respected adult. Like Kwanzaa (see p.72-7), many of these ROP programmes are re-invented rituals but draw upon major aspects of traditional African rites of passage.

In many ways the ROPs are a clear example of the enduring strength of the cultures of Africa and the Caribbean. The spirit of those forcibly shipped from Africa to the Caribbean was not crushed, in spite of the best efforts of the slavers and the plantation owners; identity with the importance of ancestorhood persists to this day, through the adoption by people in the diaspora of elements of the rites of passage of their ancestors.

Birth and naming

Nature brings the child into a social being, a corporate person. For it is the community which must protect the child, feed it, bring it up, educate it and in many other ways incorporate it into the wider community. Children are the buds of society, and every birth is the arrival of 'spring', when life shoots out and the community thrives. The birth of a child is, therefore, the concern not only of the parents but of many relatives including the living and the departed. Kinship plays an important role here, so that a child cannot be exclusively 'my child' but only 'our child'.

Birth is a time for celebration of the first major rite in the African life-cycle, initiating the new-born child into the world in a ritual and naming ceremony. Children are often protected from the dangers of the earthly world by charms or incantations; in many parts of West Africa it is common to see children covered in charms almost from the day of their birth.

Almost every African culture believes that the child has come directly from the spirit world, bringing important knowledge, talents and gifts bestowed by God, to enhance the community. Each child has an individual purpose or mission to fulfil: the family and community are charged with discovering exactly what this is.

Children wearing charms

Malidoma Patrice Somé, of the Dagara tribe of Burkina Faso, explains:

*F*OR THE DAGARA, *every person is an incarnation, that is, a spirit who has taken on a body. So our true nature is spiritual. This world is where one comes to carry out specific projects. A birth is therefore the arrival of someone, usually an ancestor that somebody already knows, who has important tasks to do here. The ancestors are the real school of the living. They are the keepers of the very wisdom the people need to live by. The life energy of ancestors who have not yet been reborn is expressed in the life of nature, in trees, mountains, rivers and still water. Grandfathers and grandmothers, therefore, are as close to an expression of ancestral energy and wisdom as the tribe can get. Consequently their interest in grandsons and granddaughters is natural. An individual who embodies a certain value would certainly be interested in anyone who came from the place where that value existed most purely. Elders become involved with a new life practically from the moment of conception because that unborn child has just come from the place they are going to.*

A few months before birth, when the grandchild is still a foetus, a ritual called a 'hearing' is held. The pregnant mother, her brothers, the grandfather, and the officiating priest are the participants. The child's father is not present for the ritual, but merely prepares the space. Afterwards, he is informed about what happened. During the ritual, the incoming soul takes the voice of the mother (some say the soul takes the whole body of the mother, which is why the mother falls into a trance and does not remember anything afterwards) and answers every question the priest asks.

The living must know who is being reborn, where the soul is from, why it chose to come here, and what gender it has chosen. Sometimes, based on the life mission of the incoming soul, the living object to the choice of gender and suggest that the opposite choice will better accommodate the role the unborn child has chosen for him- or herself. Some souls ask that specific things be made ready before their arrival – talismanic power objects, medicine bags, metal objects in the form of rings for the ankle or the wrist. They do not want to forget who they are and what they have come here to do. It is not hard to forget, because life in this world is filled with many alluring distractions. The name of the newborn is based upon the results of these communications. A name is the life programme of its bearer.

As well as a reflection of the child's task in life, or the belief that the child is the re-incarnation of an ancestor, the name given can reflect a personality trait, or indicate the time or day of the week of birth. Other circumstances surrounding the birth - such as whether it was in the dry or the rainy season, the feelings invoked by it, such as joy, or the birth-order position in the family, may also account for the choice of name. There is also a common tradition of adding names later in life, such as that of an ancestor with whom it is thought that the child shares similar personality traits.

Names from the Igbo of Nigeria include proverbs and sayings relating to how people should live their lives:

Somaadina   'Let me not exist alone'
Oraka   'The community is greater'
Adinigwe   'It is better to be better'

The Akan of Ghana give their children soul (*kra*) names based on the day of the week that they were born (natal day). Named after seven deities who assisted God in releasing the souls, it is believed that the children inherit the personality of that deity.

Deity	Name		Planet/day	Personality
	Male	**Female**		
Ayisi	Kwasi	Akosua	Sun/Sunday	pure and generous
Awo	Kwadwo or Kudwo	Adwoa	Moon/Monday	calm and peaceful
Abena	Kwabena	Abenaa	Mars/Tuesday	fierce
Aku	Kwaku	Akua	Mercury/Wednesday	wise
Abrao	Yaw	Yaa	Jupiter/Thurday	greatness
Afi	Kofi	Afua	Venus/Friday	loving
Amen	Kwame	Amma	Saturn/Saturday	mature

Name	Male/Female	Meaning	Origin
Folami	male	Respect and honour me	Yoruba
Yejide	female	Image of the mother	Yoruba
Nkruma	male/female	Ninth-born child	Akan
Ige	female	Born feet-first	Akan
Baako	male/female	First-born child	Yoruba
Abidemi	male	Born during father's absence	Yoruba
Taiwo	male/female	First-born of twins	Yoruba

For royal families only:

Name		Meaning	Origin
Adedayo		Crown become joy	Yoruba
Aderonke		Object of royal adoration	Yoruba

132

Outdooring (Naming) Ceremony of the Anlo people
from the Ewe Land of the Volta region of Ghana

*T*HE TRADITIONAL *Outdooring (naming) ceremony of the Anlo people takes place at dawn on the eighth day after the child's birth. It is the first occasion when the child is brought out of doors and presented to the world. Grandparents, aunts and uncles and adult siblings gather formally to present the baby, but until this happens, the baby is not to be taken outside. The ceremony has an*

added ritual importance as this is also the occasion when circumcision takes place if the child is a boy, and the ears are pierced if a girl.

The family gathers and the baby is brought out of doors and handed to the eldest of the grand parents, uncles or aunts. The baby is held up at arm's length in a gesture of presentation, the officiating elder offers a prayer to God Almighty and then to the ancestors committing the child to their care. The child's name is pronounced. A libation of water is poured and a drink of palm wine or liha (made from fermented corn and sweetened with sugar) is offered to everyone. The ceremony is a mixture of traditional belief, Judaism and Christianity.

This part completed, a boy is left in the hands of the male elders to be circumcised, or the female elders for ear piercing.

The baby's mother and father usually choose names, but occasionally a grandparent may choose. If the family is Christian, the Biblical name of a saint or virtue is chosen, e.g. Patience, Comfort, etc., followed by the name for the day of the week of the child's birth (Monday, Kodjo or Adjoa; Sunday, Kwasi or Akosoa etc.) and the birth position of the child is named, i.e. the third boy is Mensah and a girl is Mansah. A child can have up to four names including the surname. The third name is usually the name of an ancestor and is chosen to embody the latter's achievements and virtues.

Once the official ceremony is over, mother and baby sit outside with the family to absorb the light of the rising sun, and reminisce about the good old times, exchanging and sharing stories of ceremonies of old. If one of the names brings to mind an older relative, stories of that relative and what he or she got up to (the good things) will be shared and the wish expressed that the child will follow that example, but do even better. There will be a traditional ceremonial breakfast of chicken, lamb or goat meat prepared with roast cornmeal in palm-nut sauce.

The ceremony finishes by 9am, and during the course of the day and the next two weeks or so, friends and neighbours will call to present gifts and offer their good wishes. For the first three to six months of the baby's life, the mother will dress in white whenever she is out. The job of being a mother is regarded differently in Africa than in western cultures, as people are living communally and there are usually many members of the family who can help with the other tasks involved in running the compound, leaving the mother free so that she can concentrate on her child.

The ceremony has continued among the Anlo people here in Britain wherever there are two or more families from the same area. I remember 26 years ago when my son was born in Leeds, my Ghanaian friends of Anlo origin came together and an older family friend presided over the ceremony.

Patience Tsapko

Activities

- Think of a name which expresses your personality and your goals in life – how does it compare with the names of the Akan of Ghana?

- Compare the naming ceremonies of the Anlo with traditional naming rituals in the West, e.g. baptism.

Puberty and adulthood: initiation rites

The initiation rites of African tribes are conducted mainly at the time of the onset of puberty for both girls and boys, clearly distinguishing and acknowledging their biological and social maturation. For both sexes there is an emphasis on instilling a sense of the ideals of manhood and womanhood. This means that the 'coming of age' period of life is marked by experiences and hitherto unknown secrets which mould the young person into an adult. Helping young people to take their rightful place as productive and responsible members of the community ensures its successful continuity. None of this is left to chance. People undergoing the rites of passage associated with puberty are very carefully and systematically prepared, both morally and mentally, for all that is to follow in the next stage of their life – adulthood. The 'old' life symbolically dies and the participants in the rites are 'reborn' into the new.

This process can last for a few days or many months, but takes the form of three distinct stages. The first is one of separation from the community and the distractions of daily life, and segregation to a special, sometimes sacred area. The second phase is marked by a period of transition. The initiate experiences many changes, in such aspects as diet, clothes, and general living conditions. Boys usually undergo great hardships, and painful ordeals, including circumcision or tribal markings. They learn what it is to be an adult, about relationships with the opposite sex, the rules and taboos of their society, receive moral instruction, and gain an understanding of social responsibility and a clearer understanding of their mission or life purpose. The final phase is a joyous one, of celebration, as they are re-integrated into the community as an adult with great feasting, accompanied by drumming and masked dancing.

Many male puberty rites are carried out within the confines of secret societies. Young men are taken to 'bush schools' where they are taught the values and traditions of their particular people, as well as other life skills, by wise elders. Circumcision plays an extremely important role in the initiation, so much so that if a boy is not circumcised he is not considered to be a man, and remains an outsider in his community. This means that the boy will be denied the progression through other rites of passage, such as parenthood or holding any position of authority. During the circumcision itself, meanwhile, the boy is expected not to flinch or show any signs of pain, and only then is considered a true man or to have the potential of becoming a great warrior. Following the circumcision, the boys enjoy a period of rest and relaxation, when they are well-fed and learn the history, traditions and customs of their people, before re-joining the community for a period of celebration.

Each African people brings its youths to adulthood in different ways. Among the Bambara of Mali, boys make the transition from youth into manhood over a period of several years. Among the Diola of southern Senegal, however, initiates of Bakut have their heads shaven by male relatives, are circumcised, and subsequently have two months of teaching before they are deemed to be members of the adult population.

A particularly fascinating set of rituals accompanies boys of the Mende tribe of Sierra Leone, Guinea and Liberia in their rites of puberty. A symbolic tug of war between childhood and adulthood is enacted when initiating a young Mende man into the Poro secret society. A female member uses a piece of rope to pull him from the spirit Namu, who is said to eat him. He also undergoes tests of physical strength and suffers great hardships which teach him to accept the authority of his elders. On return to the village, he is considered 're-born', and arrives with a new name and tribal markings on his chest and back, which symbolise the teeth marks of the spirit which ate him and gave him new life. Not a great deal is known about what exactly is involved in these secret society 'schools', as participants are not allowed to tell outsiders about it. However, it is known that members of the society learn the skills necessary to live in their community: farming, building, tracking animals, shooting, the use of bush medicines and other necessary activities, as well as the oral and ceremonial folklore of their community.

Girls too, undergo their own initiation rites. Most young women grow up in the shadow of their mothers and other women, and know exactly what will be expected of them once they reach adulthood. They look forward to their initiation into adulthood, as it becomes a public expression of their womanhood and readiness for marriage.

The Sande, a female secret society in Sierra Leone, requires young girls to spend a period of six months in seclusion, under the tutelage of senior members. Amongst the camaraderie and opportunities to develop leadership skills, they learn domestic skills, the art of seduction, craft skills, and traditional forms of singing and dancing. They also learn the beliefs of their cultural group and how to honour their ancestral spirits.

The initiation ceremony of two African boys as they make the transition from boy to man

Among the Krobo ethnic group of Ghana, the Dipo Ceremony is celebrated to mark a young girl's maturity, and as a means of attracting a husband. The ceremony is observed for five days, following a three-week preparation period. A young woman is assigned a 'ritual mother' who instructs her and prepares her for her role in society, as a wife and mother. She learns to cook and maintain a home, engages in music and dance, and becomes skilled in beautifying herself. She enters the process as a child and emerges as a dignified woman. With her 'mother' she then parades through neighbouring villages performing the Dipo ceremony. She wears glass beads around her hips, and in the form of necklaces and bracelets, as a means of attracting a husband, since glass beads represent the wealth of the family and consequently make her more attractive. During this period of feasting, boys and men interested in marrying her enter into negotiations with the girl's family. Traditionally this ceremony was one that, except for the beads, was performed naked, but today a loincloth is commonplace.

Many traditional customs are no longer practised or are dying out. Female circumcision has played a major part in the female puberty rites among many African peoples, and still does so. In this cultural world, an uncircumcised woman was considered unsuitable for marriage. However, since the 1950s and 60s the efforts of women's and human rights groups have increasingly led to this practice being outlawed, as it is perceived as ritualised child abuse and a form of violence against women, with very serious health risks. Critics of this movement, however, argue that female circumcision is an integral part of their group's cultural and religious identity.

The fattening room

Another custom which has declined in use is the 'fattening' of young girls, a centuries-old rite of passage marking the transition of a young girl into womanhood. In complete contrast to the West, where female beauty and attraction are measured in the shape of slim bodies, women of the Efik tribe and others of south-eastern Nigeria endeavour to get fat to attract a husband, as their size is considered beautiful, healthy and a sign of wealth. Traditionally women would spend up to seven years in a 'fattening room', usually beginning at the age of 12.

Months before the ritual begins, the girls shave their heads and powder themselves with red dye from the camwood tree, which helps to give a good complexion. Special sacrificial rites are performed. Around their ankles or necks, they wear a number of hollow brass rings, with small stones inside, which produce sounds as they walk. On the day of entry to the room they are massaged with palm-oil and given a mat to lie on. Raffia is used to cordon off the area in which they stay and is also used as a line on which evidence of their feeding, such as meat and fish bones are hung. The mat is later replaced by a bed, and they are no longer rubbed with oil, but apply white clay to their bodies themselves. Friends come to visit and a large *calabash* is used to gather gifts.

From this point on each girl is taught the duties that will be expected of her, and the knowledge necessary to be of credit to her husband's family and to the community. Children are brought for her to look after, while their mothers work or go to market, and she is taught the etiquette and crafts of her people. In addition to this teaching, she is fed with large amounts of fattening foods, such as yams cooked in palm oil, supplied by her intended husband. She does not leave the room or exert herself in any way. It is during this time that female circumcision takes place, usually performed by her mother.

On leaving the 'fattening room' she is dressed and decorated with beads and ornaments and presented to her tribe with great rejoicing. The 'going out' ceremony is performed over a period of three days, consisting of eating, dancing and an overnight visit to her husband's home, ending with the girl being handed over to her husband by the father.

The fattening room

The fattening room is also revisited after the birth of a baby, for between three to six months. It is considered that a woman needs rest and special food to gain weight and recuperate from the rigours of childbirth. She returns to her parents' home and is not allowed to do anything other than breastfeed her baby. Her mother cares for her and massages her body with oil. On leaving, she is given gifts and a celebration takes place before she returns home to her husband.

Nowadays the length of time spent in the rooms runs to months rather than years, largely due to the cost involved. There is no clear limit as to how much weight should be gained, but the 'bigger the better' is the aspiration. Societal pressure to submit daughters to the ritual is very strong, with unfattened girls the subject of ridicule, considered to be weak representatives of a family's poverty, and therefore unable to bear children. Women are even considered to be cursed by angry gods if they do not gain weight, and will experience great difficulties as a result. Some young girls who may not be preparing for marriage may visit the rooms as simply a 'coming-of-age' ceremony, whereas mothers with young babies may return in order to gain weight. Efik women who continue their education and embark on careers might return to attend the fattening room in preparation for the marriage market.

The decline in this practice can be attributed to pressure from the West, healthier attitudes towards eating resulting from research that links the eating of too much fat to heart disease and other illnesses, and the fact that the time it takes does not fit with modern urban lifestyles. Even so, in many parts of Africa large women are still considered particularly attractive, their weight signifying the wealth of their families or husbands. This is also particularly true of the peoples which border the southern fringes of the Sahara, where some women are fattened to the extent that they cannot raise themselves without help; in these areas, where trade across the Sahara was historically of great importance and wealth is necessary to purchase the necessaries of life in a barren climate, the wealth of a potential spouse's family was always of crucial importance.

Such practices seem strange to Western eyes, but within their local contexts they are integral to the worldviews of the peoples and the environments in which they evolved their cultural practice. Rites express everything about a people's past and the way in which they engage with the world; they should not be forgotten by new generations and consigned to mere exotica, but are living and breathing aspects of daily life, expressions of vitality.

Activity

- *Write a story imagining the rites of passage of boys (for boys) or girls (for girls) in the respective secret societies of the Poro and the Sande in West Africa. Can you think of any rites of passage in your own tradition?*

Marriage

It is the point where all the members of a given community meet: the departed, the living and those yet to be born. All the dimensions of time meet here, and the whole drama of history is repeated, renewed and revitalised. Marriage is a drama in which everyone becomes an actor or actress and not just a spectator. Therefore, marriage is a duty, a requirement from the corporate society, and a rhythm of life in which everyone must participate.

John Mbiti

Ethiopian wedding ceremony

As we have seen, amongst West Africans a marriage is considered more of an alliance between two families or kinship groups than a union of two individuals. Influenced both by Islamic and local customs, many African cultures are also polygamous. This is also a legacy of the slave trade: the requirement for young men to work in plantations in the Caribbean created a sexual imbalance in African communities for which polygamy increasingly provided the solution.

Marriage customs are changing in Africa today. With growing economic problems, the bond of marriage is frequently being postponed by men, and marriage break-ups are not uncommon. Traditional views of marriage as bonding two families means that, in certain circumstances, children can be betrothed from birth. Today, however, to the dismay of elders, the infiltration of Western values has led to ideals of 'love' encroaching on traditional concepts of marriage, and many young people are breaking away and choosing their own partners.

Girls are seen as ready for marriage once they reach puberty, and it is the girl's family who will arrange the marriage. Ages at which a girl might first marry range from as young as 10 or 12 amongst the Hausa of northern Nigeria – although if she has not yet reached puberty she will remain with her parents until her first period – to the mid 20s in Senegal and Mauritania. The average age for women to marry in West Africa is around 16, reflecting both the different life expectancy and outlook from those in the West.

In contrast to the youth of their brides, however, men do not marry until they are able to support a wife – which could mean that they do not marry until they are in their 30s. In polygamous cultures such as in the Islamic regions of West Africa, men will take on as many wives as they are able to support, which can lead to very large extended families; this can also mean that, though men often do not marry until late, they can continue to contract marriages into later years.

An essential part of the marriage, among families following the Islamic faith and those following traditional African religions, is the 'bridewealth' or 'brideprice'. This is a payment in goods or cash, made by the groom with the help of his family, to the family of his future wife. It is a token of appreciation given to the bride's family, which helps to foster harmony between the two families. The amount paid is decided by negotiation, sometimes lasting several days, between the two families. Although this may seem like a financial transaction or sale, it is a symbol, similar to an engagement ring; a token of good faith. The negotiations create an opportunity for the two families meeting for the first time to interact and get to know each other. They take place at the home of the bride-to-be, in the absence of the betrothed couple, with her parents and the male relatives of the groom. The meeting will begin with friendly chat and the sharing of food and drink, which symbolises that the guests are welcomed and accepted. Later, the discussion of the brideprice, what and how much, takes place. The items and amounts vary across Africa, and from one ethnic group to another. In some countries camels, or cattle are tendered, but in many parts of West Africa, the groom's family traditionally offer *kola* nuts.

Kola are red, oval-shaped nuts with a very bitter taste which acted as a form of currency and ritual offering in Africa before colonial times. If a bundle of *kola* nuts was not given by the bridegroom's family, the wedding ceremony did not take place. Hospitality was symbolised when visitors were offered water followed by the best *kola* nuts, to show that

Nigerian wedding ceremony

they were welcome; when *kola* nuts were not offered, however, it was apparent that the visitor was not welcome. *Kola* nuts feature not only in marriage ceremonies, but also at celebrations surrounding the birth of a baby and a person's funeral, where they are distributed to all present.

Until the bride's family has received this payment and the amount is made public, no marriage takes place. The brideprice is ceremonially presented to the bride's family and the couple is considered 'engaged'. There are variations, such as in the country of Niger, where the giving of a series of gifts starts at the same time as negotiations for a possible union. Today, however, cash is more common and there is often an equal exchange of gifts between both the bride and the groom's families.

Mehndi

Also known as *Mehandi*, *Mehndi* is a traditional art form which involves decorating the body, in particular hands and feet, using a paste made from the finely ground dried leaves of the henna plant (*Lawsonia inermis*). Like a temporary tattoo, the skin is stained with intricate designs, usually for festivals and celebrations surrounding important rites of passage, such as betrothals, weddings, birth, male circumcision and religious and national holidays. The henna paste is formed by mixing the powder with either lemon juice or water. A reddish brown stain is left on the skin, which darkens over the following day. Depending on the strength of the henna, or whether substances like dye have been added, the design will last for a few weeks.

Henna has many traditional uses besides body art. For example, it is used to condition and to colour hair, and as a skin conditioner. In the East it is renowned for medicinal properties: clotting blood, healing burns and a variety of skin ailments, and in the treatment of thinning hair. It is used to make a drink that relieves stomach pain and headaches. As well as being a total sunblock, it has cooling properties, useful in reducing swelling, and people are known to apply the paste without any pattern, or to simply step into it, sometimes called a 'henna-shoe'.

Traditional designs vary, but they fall into three distinct groupings. Middle Eastern designs, which tend not to cover the whole area of the hand or foot, are mainly beautiful floral patterns, with leaves and vines, similar to those found on Arabic textiles, paintings and carvings. Indian and Pakistani designs, which tend to cover more of the hand and feet, are usually very intricate and thus time-consuming to produce, in the form of floral and paisley patterns, teardrop shapes and fine lines. Hindu designs might depict birds such as peacocks, whereas Muslim designs will be devoid of representative art. North African designs are large, bold, geometrical patterns, with lots of lines, dots and blocks of colour, following the shape of the hand. Some designs involve blocks of colour on the tips of fingers and toes, including nails. Followers of almost all of the main religions of the world, Christians, Muslims, Jews, Hindus, and other religions, use henna in their celebrations.

In many cultures across the world, natural red substances such as blood and ochre have spiritual significance. Henna fits this pattern. It has also been endowed with magical symbolism. It is purported to enhance fertility and femininity and protect from the 'evil eye'. In Morocco, doors of new homes are often painted with henna to bring prosperity and keep evil at bay. Pregnant mothers are painted with henna symbols by *hannayas* in their seventh month to protect them and their babies, and once the umbilical cord is cut, a henna paste is applied to the belly button to ensure health and prosperity. It is also used to protect bulls, cows and horses, by decorating their foreheads. Tombstones, too, are sometimes washed with henna in order to please the spirits.

Today, the art form is used across the continent of Africa, as well as in India and the Middle East, and the parts of the world in which the descendants from these areas have settled. Traditional *Mehndi* designs have been complemented by those from other cultures such as Celtic designs and Chinese symbols. Moreover, henna is mixed with the leaves of other plants and substances such as indigo, tea, coffee, sugar, tamarind, lemon, lime, and clove or eucalyptus oils, to create more vibrant and longer-lasting designs. *Mehndi* can be bought in tubes, but is mainly applied using cones, similar to those used in cake decoration. For those lacking in artistic confidence, stencils can be purchased.

opportunity of bride and groom to become close on the wedding night as the groom seeks his name amongst the designs. Application and drying time can take up to five hours. Tradition states that a mother-in-law will love her daughter-in-law more the darker her *mehndi* is. This may have some truth as it requires a great deal of patience to sit still for such a length of time, patience being a useful virtue for a new wife. Another reason for ensuring a long-lasting *mehndi* is that the new bride is not expected to do any housework until her *mehndi* has worn off.

In Africa, a henna party or ceremony preceding a wedding is somewhat like a hen night before a western wedding. The bride-to-be and her female relatives and close friends gather to enjoy each others' company, to eat food and sing or listen to music. It is traditionally held the night before the wedding, although it can be a few days before, at the home of the bride. The main focus of the evening is to apply *mehndi* to the bride's hand and feet. The guests may also have *mehndi* applied, but most care and precision in design is taken with the bride, who must be the most beautiful. The groom's name or initials may be carefully hidden within the design, which becomes part of the

146

Activities

- *Look at different Mehndi designs. Choose a style and create a pattern in that style on the templates provided on p.166-7.*

- *Create your own individual Mehndi design. Write a paragraph about your inspiration.*

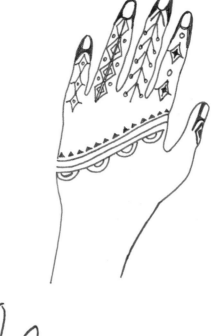

A new bride has a very special position in all African communities, and she is treated with great respect. She is the link between the ancestors and the unborn child, and is therefore seen as carrying the potential for rebirth from the spirit world, from which all great ancestors are reborn. She has the potential, therefore, of being the mother of a chief, a warrior or an elder.

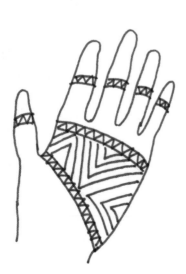

Given the fact that polygamous homes are common in Africa, the new bride will often find herself entering into a household where there are already other wives. This creates a different social situation from marriage in the West. Traditionally, the number of wives and children a man had was a means by which he could accumulate more wealth and status. More wives meant more children, more workers, and the means to acquire more wealth. Though women are brought up knowing that this is the system that they will enter, problems often arise, such as jealousy between the wives; though at first senior wives can pull rank, the favouring of junior wives by their husbands can create all kinds of problems which are difficult to resolve. Children tend to identify themselves partly by whether or not they have the same mother, and this can lead to conflicts within the family compound according to the wealth and status of different mothers' families. On the other hand, the existence of a large household means that there is less work for each wife to do.

In these complex and large family groups divorce is common for a number of reasons. It occurs mainly if the wife 'repudiates' or refuses to recognise the marriage. In these circumstances, the brideprice her husband paid will need to be repaid, and in Islamic West Africa a woman will be expected to remarry quickly, within a few months, once her *idda* (a 40-day waiting period as set out in the Qu'ran) is observed, if she is still of child-bearing age.

'Jumping the Broom' – One, Two, Three... Jump!

In the Caribbean, the practice of slavery distorted the traditional aspects of marriage that slaves brought with them from Africa, and especially the idea that marriage represented the coming together of two families. Slaves in the plantations were usually kept apart from members of the same ethnic group and therefore it was impossible to maintain a sense of family lines being joined together in marriage, as slaves came from such different regions of Africa.

The slave-owners, meanwhile, did not see the marriage of slaves in anything but a pragmatic light. Young male and female slaves were encouraged to 'couple' for the mere purpose of having children, and maintaining the workforce. Slave-owners and plantation overseers were quick to eradicate many rituals and other aspects of cultural heritage that were transported to the Americas with the slaves. Some of these, however, were considered harmless and were allowed to continue and one such tradition was that which came to be known as 'Jumping the Broom'.

Often wrongly considered to be a 're-invented' ritual, 'Jumping the Broom' can be traced back through slave narratives to the early days of slavery. It is believed to have been adapted from a tribal marriage ritual, still practised in some areas of West Africa, which involved jumping over a line or sticks on the ground representing the new home of the bride and groom. Crossing the line signified a new start for the couple, as they began their married life together. In the New World, the broom, a positive symbol of domestic life, was chosen both symbolically and spiritually to represent a 'new' beginning, in a new family, the 'old' being swept away.

Increasingly, many African-Americans incorporate this traditional ritual into their modern wedding ceremonies as a way of honouring their ancestry, and elaborately decorated brooms can be purchased for the purpose. It is performed either after the minister declares the couple to be 'husband and wife', or at the Reception, as the bridal party enter.

During the ceremony, guests are asked to form a circle around the bride and groom, with the broom placed on the floor in front of them. The symbolism of the ceremony is explained: that it signifies the coming together of the couple and their families, and the request for the community's support for the union. While

these words are spoken, the couple hold the broom and brush the floor within the circle. The groom then takes the broom and places it on the floor. He takes the hand of his bride, and everyone counts, 'One, Two, Three… Jump!'

Activity

- As a class, create and perform your own 'Jumping the Broom' ceremony

'Jumping the broom'

Death and ancestorhood

Many African societies believe that their communities are composed of three specific groups: the living, the ancestors whom the living join when they die, and those waiting to be born. The bonds between these groups, humans and spirits, underlie the 'cycle of life' and the strengths of families and communities. There is a connection always between the dead and the living, but there are distinctions also between categories of spirits. Some are simply dead relatives, others are ancestors, revered and respected elders, who have died and taken with them into the spirit world the same high status they had in life. Shrines to the ancestral spirits are a constant reminder of the importance of rituals and traditions, showing respect for the leadership and guidance given by an elder whilst he was living. The dead elder is still an integral part of the family and community, called upon for advice and protection.

As with cultures all over the world, in Africa there are a large variety of customs associated with death and burial. Most burial rites are concerned with ensuring that the spirit of the dead person will have all the necessary equipment he needs to join the other spirit-relatives, and that care is taken to bury the body in the correct manner and place. Some bodies are buried near or underneath the house, whereas other ethnic groups bury them far away. Most burials have to take place quickly due to the hot climate. But some time after the funeral, weeks, months or even years later, friends and relatives gather and perform rituals to help the transition of the soul to the spiritual world from where it originated, and to prevent it from wandering and haunting the living. In one such ritual, the Xhosa of South Africa perform what is called Ukukhapha, during which the living spiritually accompany the dead to the spirit world, reminding them to remember those left behind. They also have another called Ukubiyisa ('bringing back'), which ensures that the individual spiritually returns to live among his people and protect them.

In some circumstances, the dead are feared even more than the gods. They exert great power over the social life of the community. They may constitute the head of the family or clan, and in death have more powers than when they were living. Their will is made known through dreams and visions, or in messages mediated by special members of the community. They return to live again, re-born as babies in the family. Illnesses and accidents are attributed to their displeasure, but, by the same token, they can be appeased and thereby provide a cure for these ills. Crops and the harvest are their concern, as is the weather which affects a successful harvest, and so there are many family prayers and a host of ceremonies which call for their intervention. All family property belongs to them and they must be consulted before any major decisions are made about it, usually by casting lots or throwing nuts on the floor. From the pattern in which they fall, an answer is concluded.

Nowhere is the influence and importance of the dead more starkly seen than in the art of Africa. In masks, carvings and sculptures, the ancestors, animals and other powerful beings are portrayed as both fearful and calming influences; most of these objects are abstract in design, however, denoting that the scope of the dead is beyond the imagination of the living. In ceremonies that regularly occur in most communities, the masked figures featured represent the living dead, and speak quite clearly, giving messages and warnings to the living.

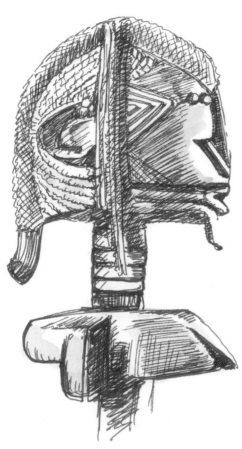

Sculptures and carvings

This again shows how every aspect
of culture in African communities is
interconnected. The masquerades
which were discussed earlier (see
p.90) thus have a direct connection
not only to celebrations but to the
other worlds which interact with
our own.

Death rituals in the Caribbean

In the Caribbean, rituals associated with death have evolved differently from the rituals of Africa. Death is viewed as a time when malevolent *duppies* are most likely to be released, and when these spirits could significantly affect the lives of the living (see more on *duppies* below). A large number of rituals have therefore developed, to ensure a smooth passage from this world to the next. As in Africa, these rituals also indicate a great deal of respect for the dead. However, in the Caribbean today, only the older generation and those living in more rural areas observe most of these rituals.

An example of old Caribbean death rituals comes from Carriacou, where the Tombstone Feast is a ritual that maintains respect for ancestors, bringing back generations of a family from wherever they have settled in the world. Here, following the death, there are a number of gatherings called Prayer Meetings or Prayer Nights, which take place on the 3rd, 9th and 40th nights. One of the last two of these celebrations will feature a Big Drum dance. On the first anniversary of the death there is a mass, usually in the morning, followed by refreshments, and a table is set at the home of the deceased in the evening. Somewhere between the 2nd and 3rd year after the death, the headstone is placed on the grave and a huge celebration takes place: a 'ground-wetting' (libation) ritual takes place, as does the sharing of traditional food, the drinking of rum, storytelling and dancing. Again a table is set for the deceased, and food is placed on the grave. This means that when the headstone is placed on the grave of the deceased, it is the final element in a series of rituals associated with death and burial which take place over three years, and which are remembered annually by those who are able to attend. It is believed that the spirit of the deceased will not rest in peace until the stone is placed.

Another example of long-standing Caribbean death rituals can be found in Jamaica. Here, the idea that the dead have great powers and can return and haunt the living is very evident, and the following death rituals used to be observed:

- In order for the dead not to return to haunt their family members, everyone had to say their goodbyes to the corpse.

- Once life had left the body, two members of the family would wash it, one beginning at the head and the other at the feet, and meeting in the middle.

- The water used to wash the body would be saved and poured into the grave.

- Mirrors would be turned against walls to stop reflections that could bring more deaths.

- The house would be swept out with new palm brooms.

- The clothes of the deceased would be given away or burnt.

- If the person had died in bed, the body would be turned so that the head faced the foot of the bed, to confuse any *duppies* that might be in the vicinity.

- Once the corpse was taken from the house the mattress might be turned over, or burnt, or the bed would be left outdoors for three days to rid it of any lurking negative spiritual residues.

Obeah

Derived from the Ashanti term *obayi*, meaning a malicious spirit, Obeah is a type of witchcraft or spiritual power which can influence all kinds of events, in either a positive or negative way. For example, it could be used to bring good fortune, to exact revenge, or to cure an ailment. Ghosts, shadows of the dead, or *duppies* also form part of this belief. Many people regard these beliefs as superstitious nonsense, but they are taken very seriously by a large number of people of African heritage in the Caribbean and elsewhere in the world. In Jamaica, the practice of Obeah is outlawed, although there are very few prosecutions.

Obeah-men are paid to either place or remove curses on subjects, usually in the form of rituals, charms and, more commonly bags containing powders ('powders of compliance') which, when sprinkled on the subject, bring about the desired result. These curses can only be removed by a more powerful Obeah-man. There is much of this practice that is reminiscent of cultural practice in Africa; in many parts of West Africa today powders are also sprinkled to obtain a desired spiritual or magical effect.

Good Obeah-men, often known as *myalmen*, perform ceremonies to counteract bad obeah. *Myalmen* are often respected members of the community in rural areas who prescribe African herbal medicines for a range of both physical and spiritual ailments. Through the 'shadow-catching' ceremony held around the roots of silk cotton trees, they are supposed to be able to catch duppies. They also play an important role in ceremonies to mark births, illness and death, when spirits are believed to be active.

I Like to Stay Up

I like to stay up
and listen
when big people talking
jumbie stories

I does feel
so tingly and excited
inside me

But when my mother say
'Girl, time for bed'

Then is when
I does feel a dread

Then is when
I does jump into me bed

Then is when
I does cover up
from me feet to me head

Then is when
I does wish I didn't listen
to no stupid jumbie story

Then is when I does wish I did read
me book instead

Grace Nichols

Jumbie, Jumbie - African chant

Jumbie, Jumbie, drying the slate
Jumbie, Jumbie, drying the slate
Jumbie, Jumbie gimme the dry and take the wet
(BLOW)

Some children use a small slate to write on for their lessons. Between lessons they must sprinkle it with water to erase the previous lesson's work. As it takes a long time to dry they ask the help of *Jumbie*, a friendly, sometimes mischievous Caribbean ghost.

153

A *duppy*, from the African word *dupe* or *dube* meaning 'spirit of the dead', also called a jumby, is the name given to a supernatural being or ghost. The belief, stemming from Africa, is that when someone dies his or her body goes into the ground, the soul returns to God, but the spirit stays in the temporal world and is susceptible to the manipulation of the Obeah-man to do good or evil to the living. If well treated, the spirit can bring good fortune and even help to predict the future, but if it is ignored or treated badly, it will bring illness or bad luck. It possesses all the attributes it had when it was alive - it can eat, drink, talk and display good or bad behaviour. Moreover it likes its name to be given to a child of the same sex, hence many people in the Caribbean are known throughout their lifetime by a 'jumby name' as well as their formal name.

In Jamaica, there is a popular superstition that encourages individuals to carry a supply of stones or matches with them when walking alone at night. These should be dropped to confuse any duppy in the vicinity, who will not be able to count beyond three, and will be confined to the spot eternally.

The anthropologist Zora Neale Hurston studied Obeah and duppies in Haiti and Jamaica in 1938, by attending and observing many ceremonies and rituals. She found that Jamaicans believed that duppies lived in silk-cotton trees and almond trees, and therefore neither of these trees should be planted too close a house. After observing a 'nine nights' ceremony, she wrote (in *Tell My Horse: Voodoo and Life in Haiti and Jamaica*):

IT ALL STEMS from the firm belief in survival after death. Or rather that there is no death. Activities are merely changed from one condition to the other. One old man smoking jackass rope tobacco said to me in explanation: 'One day you see a man walking the road, the next day you come to his yard and find him dead. Him don't walk, him don't talk again. He is still and silent and does none of the things that he used to do. But you look upon him and you see that he has all the parts that the living have. Why is it that he cannot do what the living do? It is because the thing that gave power to these parts is no longer there. That is the duppy, and that is the most powerful part of any man. Everybody has evil in them, and when a man is alive, the heart and the brain controls him and he will not abandon himself to many evil things. But when the duppy leaves the body, it no longer has anything to restrain it and it will do more terrible things than any man ever dreamed of. It is not good for a duppy to stay among living folk. The duppy is much too powerful and is apt to hurt people all the time. So we make nine night to force the duppy to stay in his grave.

As well as the duppies of ordinary people, there are a range of other spirits who can be found in children's bedtime stories and are an integral part of the folklore and culture of the Caribbean islands, such as *Ol' Higue* (Jamaica and Guyana, also known as *Soucouyant* in Trinidad and Grenada, and Hag in Barbados), *River Mumma, Rolling Calf, Whistling Cowboy, Three-Foot Horse* (Jamaica), *La Diablesse, Douen, PapaBois* (Trinidad) and *Loop Garoo* (Grenada).

Nine Night ceremonies

Similar to a wake, Nine Night is an old folk custom which is still observed in a variety of forms in many parts of Jamaica. Traditionally, the ceremony takes place on the ninth night after the burial at the home of the deceased; this is the final religious social gathering of the family of the deceased, and its principal purpose is to bid farewell to the soul.

The ceremony is conducted by someone highly respected in the community who leads the hymn-singing, calling out a line or two of the song which is then either repeated or continued by the others who are present. At this time a particularly lively chorus called a *Sankey* is also sung. Amidst the singing, Bible passages are read. Though there may be some variation across the island, certain common elements are generally practised. There is praying, the playing of games such as dominoes, storytelling and the telling of riddles. All of this takes place in the room in which the person died.

In areas where there is a strong link with Revivalism, a three-tiered altar is made on a table in the room. An equal number of black and white candles and a glass of water are placed on each level, and a vase of flowers and a photograph (if available) of the deceased person is placed on the top. Just before midnight, all those gathered light the candles and make short speeches about the deceased. Whether the person was popular or not, only good comments are allowed as a sign of respect. The person officiating then calls out the deceased person's name three times and tells his or her life story. At midnight it is believed that the spirit will possess someone in the room, and through this medium will determine unresolved issues, such as the division of property, or the identification of a murderer if the death was not from natural causes. If the spirit does not arrive at the appointed time, then an appearance is encouraged by the throwing of frankincense and myrrh onto burning coals, placed on ashes in a pan. When this is over, all those gathered march from the house singing 'Rock of Ages' or some similar hymn.

At this point food is generally distributed. 'Chocolate tea' or coffee, rum, fried fish and hard dough bread are popular items on these occasions. Sometimes unsalted rice (it is believed that spirits do not eat salt) and rum are sprinkled on the ground for the dead person.

The ceremony continues until daybreak with more singing and playing of games. The next morning, rituals are performed to ensure that the dead person has left the home.

'Sankeys' were so-called after a man named Ira D. Sankey (1840-1908), a talented singer and songwriter. He travelled extensively in North America and Britain with the evangelist preacher Dwight L. Moody, who changed the face of music played in churches by popularising hymns with modern lyrics. He wrote short, simple gospel songs, with refrains or choruses, in the style of popular music of his day. He also set poems to music: the most famous being a poem written by Elizabeth C Clephane, called 'The Ninety and Nine' (1868) based on the Bible passages about the 'Good Shepherd' found in Matthew 18:13, Luke 15:6, and John 10:14. At first his work caused great controversy, as traditionally hymns were very staid, and solidly based on Bible scripture. However Sankeys later became popular all over the world.

The Ninety and Nine

*There were ninety and nine that safely lay
In the shelter of the fold;
But one was out on the hills away,
Far off from the gates of gold.
Away on the mountains wild and bare;
Away from the tender Shepherd's care.*

*'Lord, Thou hast here Thy ninety and nine;
Are they not enough for Thee?'
But the Shepherd made answer: 'This of Mine
Has wandered away from Me.
And although the road be rough and steep,
I go to the desert to find My sheep.'*

*But none of the ransomed ever knew
How deep were the waters crossed;
Nor how dark was the night the Lord passed
    through
Ere He found His sheep that was lost.
Out in the desert He heard its cry;
'Twas sick and helpless and ready to die.*

*'Lord, whence are those blood-drops all the way,
That mark out the mountain's track?'
'They were shed for one who had gone astray
Ere the Shepherd could bring him back.'
'Lord, whence are Thy hands so rent and torn?'
'They're pierced tonight by many a thorn.'*

*And all through the mountains, thunder-riv'n,
And up from the rocky steep,
There arose a glad cry to the gate of heav'n,
'Rejoice! I have found My sheep!'
And the angels echoed around the throne,
'Rejoice, for the Lord brings back His own!'*

Words by Elizabeth C Clephane
and music by Ira Sankey

Nine Nights is often confused with a Set-up which is observed before the burial. This might last many nights and involves the friends and relatives of the deceased 'setting up' together to mourn, share memories and celebrate the life of the deceased person. It is believed that this gives the dead person a good send-off from this world and ensures that their duppy does not return to haunt the living. Those present cook and eat food, drink rum, share stories and riddles, sing songs, play ring games and dance traditional dances. Inevitably this has also served as a means of preserving a great deal of folk culture.

In Britain today, this custom is still observed by those who came and settled here in the post-war period, though it has taken on a slightly different form. Friends and relatives begin to gather at the home of the deceased from the day of the death, and the whole event normally lasts until the night of the funeral. Music is performed, food and drink are liberally provided, dominoes are played, memories are shared and there is often much laughter. To an outsider, it resembles a party and can seem quite insensitive considering that a grieving family is also present.

Hyacinth Lewis: Nine Nights ceremonies in Jamaica

*A*s a child, *in Jamaica, I grew up seeing my family and the community keeping up 'Nine Nights' or 'Nine Night', as we called it. This was always after someone in our village or the surrounding villages had died.*

When someone died, his or her body would be kept in the house until the next day and then buried. Because of the heat, there was no way the body could be kept any longer!

The first night was called the 'Set-up', and people would come to the house where the person died. The men would carry with them their own mugs, and they would also have with them song books, dominoes, cards, rum, soft drinks and board, to make the coffin. The ladies would take with them bread, sugar, coffee, tea and chocolate. They would be responsible for making hot drinks through the night until the next morning, while the men made the coffin. The others played games and sang songs, whilst children slept or played games.

The next morning, people would go to their homes, wash, change and come back for the funeral. The men would then bring with them: yams, green bananas, breadfruit, and anything else they have as food in the field. Some would even kill a pig or a goat and bring some of the meat. The ladies would have with them: rice, flour, oil, seasonings, plates, knives and forks, etc. The part the children would play would be to go fetch the water, go to the shops for whatever they needed, and wash the dishes.

Some of the ladies would be cooking, whilst others would be washing the body of the dead person and dressing it. The men would be digging the grave, which in most cases would be very close to the house, and whilst they were doing this they would be drinking more rum.

After all this was done, the body would be placed in the coffin by the men, and then carried on their shoulders to the church where you would have crowds of people following and singing.

Some of the ladies would stay home, cook and get tables ready with the food. After the service in the church, the men would then carry the body back to be buried. Then everyone would eat and drink!

When this was all over, some would go, others would stay, but at night they would all come again, even others who had just heard about the death, and do the same things: eat, drink, tell stories, play games, sing songs. This would continue for nine nights.

Nine Night gathering ceremony

Activities

- *List the rites of passage celebrated in your family and community, and write about the rituals that take place with each one. Are there any similarities or differences with those celebrated by children in your class from a different ethnic background?*

- *Hold a class discussion about whether you think rites of passage are important.*

- *Create your own rite of passage celebration. Design a programme for the ceremony.*

- *Research some other 'Sankeys'. Find the music score and sing one in your classroom.*

Appendix

Adinkra and Mehndi Patterns

Adinkra symbols and meanings

Akoben

war horn

vigilance, wariness

Epa

handcuffs

law, justice, slavery

Akoma

the heart

patience and tolerance

Gye nyame

except for God

supremacy of God

Aya

fern

endurance,
resourcefulness

Hwemudua

measuring stick

examination, quality
control

Denkyem

crocodile

adaptability

Kintinkantan

puffed up extravagance

arrogance, extravagance

Duafe

wooden comb

beauty, hygiene, feminine
qualities

Mframadan

wind-resistant house

fortitude, preparedness

Nkyinkyim

twistings

initiative, dynamism, versatility

Osramne nsoromma

the moon and the star

love, faithfulness, harmony

Nsoromma

child of the heavens

guardianship

Owuo atwedee

the ladder of death

mortality

Nyame biribi wo soro

God is in the heavens

hope

Sankofa

return and get it

learn from the past

Nyame nnwu na mawu

God never dies, therefore I cannot die

life after death

Sankofa
(alternative version)
return and get it

learn from the past

Nyame nti

by God's grace

faith and trust in God

Mehndi patterns

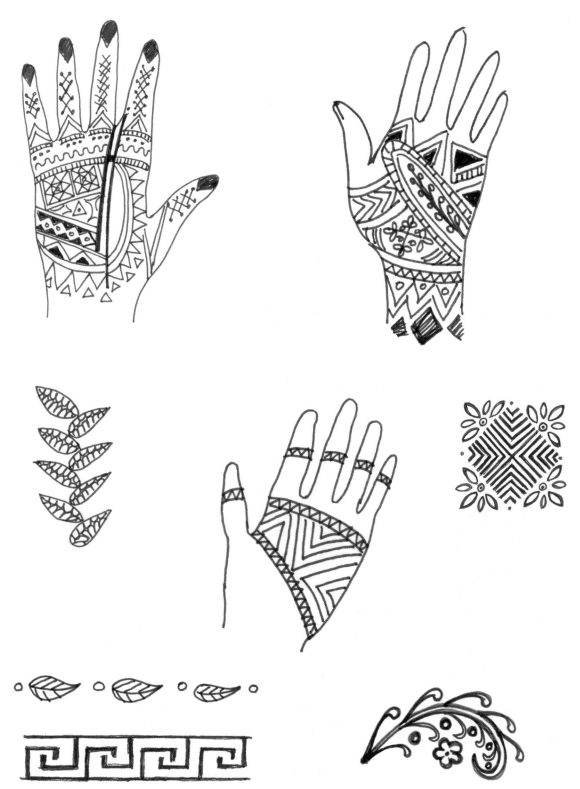

Hand template

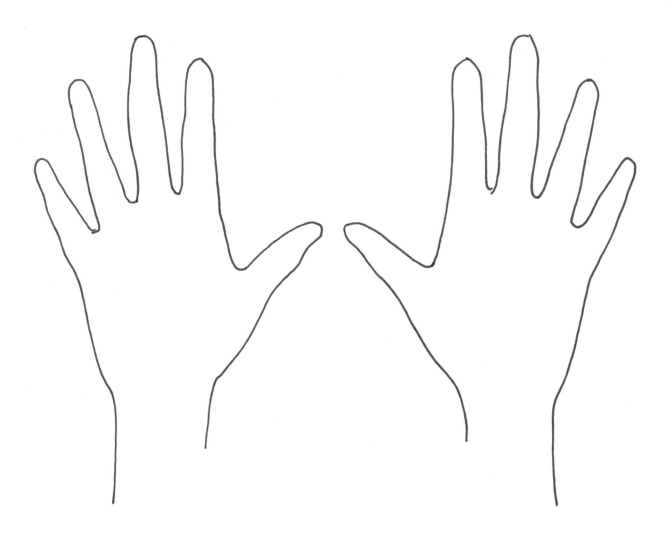

Foot template

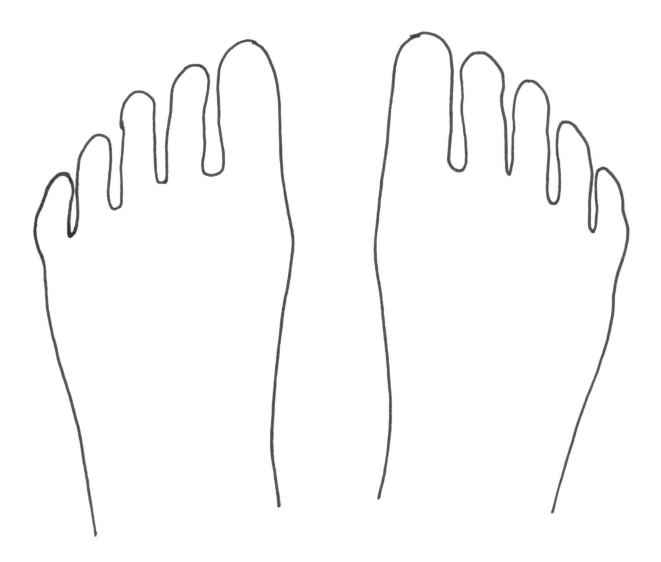

Endnotes

Section Two: Festivals and Food

1. From *Mantra's Multicultural Book of Songs*, edited by Misha Chadha

2. From *African & Caribbean Resource Pack*

3. Full words and music at: www.jamaicans.com/culture/folk/linstead/s html

4. No. 33 in *Mango Spice: 44 Caribbean songs*, chosen by Yvonne Conolly, Gloria Cameron and Sonia Singham

Section Three: Music, Dance and the Oral Tradition

5. From *The Art of African Masks*, by Carol Finley

6. From *Anancy and Miss Lou*, by Louise Bennett

7. No. 40 in *Mango Spice: 44 Caribbean songs*, chosen by Yvonne Conolly, Gloria Cameron and Sonia Singham

Bibliography and further reading

Historical Background

Carretta, V. (ed.) *Olaudah Equiano: The Interesting Narrative and other writings*, London, Penguin Books, 1995

Claypole, M., and Robottom, J., *Caribbean Story, Book One: Foundations*, Harlow, Longman Caribbean, 1980

Greene, M., *Slave Young, Slave Long: the American Slave Experience*, Minneapolis, Lerner Publications Company, 1999

Haley, A., *Roots: The Saga of an American Family*, New York, Doubleday Publishing, 1976

Hall, D., *The Caribbean Experience: An Historical Survey 1450 -1960*, Oxford, Heineman, 1982

James, C. L. R., *The Black Jacobins*, London, Allison and Busby, 1980

Mathurin, L., *The Rebel Woman in the British West Indies during Slavery*, Kingston, Institute of Jamaica, 1975

Parkinson, W., *This Gilded African: Toussaint L'Ouverture*, London, Quartet Books Ltd., 1980

Festivals and Food

Achebe, C., *Things Fall Apart*, London, Heinemann, 1958

Barrett, L., *The Sun and the Drum: African Roots in Jamaican Folk Tradition*, London, Heineman, 1976

Benghiat, N., *Traditional Jamaican Cookery*, London, Penguin, 1985

Bethel, C., and Bethel, N., *Junkanoo: Festival of the Bahamas*, Macmillan Education Ltd., London and Basingstoke, 1991

Inquai, T., *A Taste of Africa*, Trenton, African World Press, 1998

Janzan, K., *The ABC of Creative Caribbean Cookery*, London, Macmillan Education Ltd, 1994

Newton Chocolate, D., *Kwanzaa*, Chicago, IL, Children's Press, 1990

Recipes: Cooking of the Caribbean Islands, London, Macmillan Education Ltd., 1985.

Music, Dance and the Oral Tradition

Barrett, Sr., L., *The Rastafarians*, Boston, Beacon Press, 1988

Barrett, L., *The Sun and the Drum: African Roots in Jamaican Folk Tradition*, London, Heineman, 1976

Bennett, L., *Anancy and Miss Lou*, Kingston, Sangster's Book Stores Ltd., 1979

Chadha, M., *Mantra's Multicultural Book of Songs*, London, Mantra Lingua Ltd., 1994

Connolly, Y., Cameron, G., and Singham, S., *Mango Spice: 44 Caribbean Songs*, London, A. and C. Black, 1981

Courlander, H., *A Treasury of Afro-American Folklore*, New York, Marlow and Company, 1996

Finley, C., *The Art of African Masks*, Minneapolis, Lerner Publications Co., 1999

Grant, C., *Ring of Steel: pan sound and symbol*, London, Macmillan Education, 1995

Kebede, A., *Roots of Black Music: The Vocal, Instrumental, and Dance Heritage of Africa and Black America*, Trenton, Africa World Press, 1995

Knappert, J., *The A-Z of African Proverbs*, London, Karnak House, 1989

Niane, D.T., *Sundiata: An Epic of Old Mali*, Addison-Wesley Pub. Co., 1995

Nichols, G., *I like that stuff*, Curtis Brown
  Group Ltd., 1984
Noel, T., *The Steelband from Bamboo to Pan*,
  London, Commonwealth Institute
Salkey, A., *Tales of the Caribbean*, Ginn and
  Company Ltd., 1985
Sherlock, P., *Anansi the Spiderman*, London,
  Macmillan Education, 1995
Wisniewski, D., *Sundiata: The Lion King*,
  New York, Clarion Books, 1992
Zephaniah, B., *The Dread Affair: Collected
  Poems*, London, Arrow Books, 1985

Rites of Passage

Hurston, Z. N., *Tell My Horse: Voodoo and Life
  in Haiti and Jamaica*, New York,
  HarperCollins, 1980
Laye, C., *The African Child*, Glasgow,
  Fontana/Collins, 1977

Mbiti, J., *African Religions and Philosophy*,
  Oxford, Heineman, 1969
Somé, M.S., *Of Water and the Spirit*, New
  York, Arkana, 1995

Useful websites

www.africanhistory.about.com
www.jamaicans.com
www.black-history-month.co.uk
www.jcdc.org.jm
www.officialkwanzaawebsite.org
www.oware.org
www.hennapage.com
www.blackheritagetodayuk.co.uk

Index

About the author

Gail Johnson was born in England and is of mixed heritage parentage: Jamaican father and English mother. She works as a teacher at a children's centre in Gloucester. She has a passion for recording history, particularly that of Caribbean community members who have settled in Gloucestershire. In 2001 she was awarded an OBE for Services to Education in Gloucestershire. She has two daughters, Kathryn and Sara.

Other books by Hawthorn Press

Festivals Together
Guide to multicultural celebration

SUE FITZJOHN, MINDA WESTON, JUDY LARGE

This resource guide for celebration introduces a selection of 26 Buddhist, Christian, Hindu, Jewish, Muslim and Sikh festivals. It offers a lively introduction to the wealth of different ways of life. There are stories, things to make, recipes, songs, customs and activities for each festival, comprehensively illustrated.

224pp; 250 x 200mm; paperback; 978-1-869890-46-9

Festivals, Family and Food
Guide to seasonal celebration

DIANA CAREY AND JUDY LARGE

This family favourite is a unique, well loved source of stories, recipes, things to make, activities, poems, songs and festivals. Each festival such as Christmas, Candlemas and Martinmas has its own, well illustrated chapter. There are also sections on Birthdays, Rainy Days, Convalescence and a birthday Calendar. The perfect present for a family, it explores the numerous festivals that children love celebrating.

224pp; 250 x 200mm; paperback; 978-0-950706-23-8

The Islamic Year
Surahs, Stories and Celebrations

NOORAH AL-GAILANI AND CHRIS SMITH

Celebrate the Islamic Year in your family or at school! You are invited to explore Muslim festivals with this inspiring treasury of stories, surahs, songs, games, recipes, craft and art activities. The Islamic Year is beautifully illustrated with traditional patterns, maps and pictures drawn from many parts of the Muslim world, and Arabic calligraphy.

240pp; 250 x 200mm; paperback; 978-1-903458-14-3

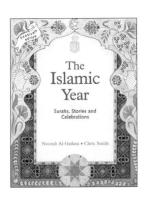

Jabulani!
Ideas for making music

CAROL SHEPHARD AND BOBBIE STORMONT

Everything you need to enjoy creating music – without having to read music or follow a song-sheet. Find your voice with chants and raps, write your own songs, and celebrate rhythm with marching, finger clicks, clapping and rumble games.

This user-friendly guide and CD is suitable for all ages and abilities, including those with special needs.

128pp; 246 x 189mm; paperback/cd; 978-1-903458-51-8

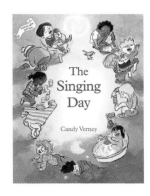

The Singing Day
Songbook and CD for singing with young children

CANDY VERNEY

Singing with babies is one of the joys of being a parent. It is a lifetime gift from you that children love. This easy to use songbook and CD offer practical help for singing with young children from birth to 4 years old.

160pp; 250 x 200mm; paperback/cd; 978-1-903458-25-9

The Singing Year
Songbook and CD for singing with young children

CANDY VERNEY

The *Singing Year* follows a child's journey through the cycle of the seasons with an exuberant collection of music, songs and poems. Each season includes ideas for activities to accompany the songs: plants for the family garden, and games and crafts using nature's bounty. For the non-musical, there are plenty of practical hints and techniques to build your confidence as a singer, and a CD so that you can hear all the songs in action.

160pp; 250 x 200mm; paperback/cd; 978-1-903458-39-6

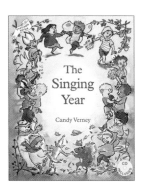

Ordering books

If you have difficulties ordering Hawthorn Press books from a bookshop, you can order direct from:

United Kingdom

Booksource
50 Cambuslang Road, Cambuslang, Glasgow
G32 8NB
Tel: 0845 370 0063
Fax: 0845 370 0064
E-mail: orders@booksource.net

USA/North America

Steiner Books
PO Box 960, Herndon
VA 20172-0960
Tel: (800) 856 8664
Fax: (703) 661 1501
E-mail: service@steinerbooks.org

Dear Reader

If you wish to follow up your reading of this book, please tick the boxes below as appropriate, fill in your name and address and return to Hawthorn Press:

☐ Please send me a catalogue of other Hawthorn Press books.

☐ Please send me details of Festivals events and courses.

Questions I have about *Festivals* are:

Name _____

Address _____

_____

_____

_____

Postcode _____ Tel. no. _____

Please return to: Hawthorn Press, Hawthorn House,

1 Lansdown Lane, Stroud, Glos. GL5 1BJ, UK

or Fax (01453) 751138